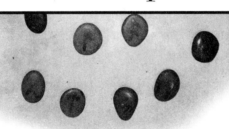

Gods of the Runes

The Divine Shapers of Fate

Frank Joseph

Illustrated by Ian Daniels

Bear & Company
Rochester, Vermont • Toronto, Canada

Bear & Company
One Park Street
Rochester, Vermont 05767
www.BearandCompanyBooks.com

Text paper is SFI certified

Bear & Company is a division of Inner Traditions International

Library of Congress Cataloging-in-Publication Data

Joseph, Frank.
  Gods of the runes : the divine shapers of fate / Frank Joseph ; illustrated by Ian
Daniels.
      p. cm.
  Summary: "The ancient origins and divinatory power of the runes"—Provided by
publisher.
  Includes bibliographical references (p.   ) and index.
  ISBN 978-1-59143-116-9
  1. Runes—Miscellanea. 2. Gods, Norse—Miscellanea. 3. Divination. I. Title.
  BF1779.R86J572 2010
  133.3'3—dc22
                                                                2010031886

Printed and bound in the United States by Lake Book Manufacturing
The text paper is SFI certified. The Sustainable Forestry Initiative® program
promotes sustainable forest management.

10 9 8 7 6 5 4 3 2 1

Text design and layout by Jon Desautels
This book was typeset in Garaond Premier Pro with Arepo used as a display
typeface

To send correspondence to the author of this book, mail a first-class letter to the
author c/o Inner Traditions • Bear & Company, One Park Street, Rochester, VT
05767, and we will forward the communication.

Contents

The Runes Are Spiritual Touchstones

I have known and admired the author Frank Joseph for many years, dating back to a time when I worked for Llewellyn Publications and helped him promote his very first book there in 1992: *Sacred Sites: A Guidebook to Sacred Centers and Mysterious Places in the United States.* What I observed in him was a painstaking attention to detailed research and a lifelong passion for exploring and unraveling ancient mysteries of myth and magic. Frank would assemble his slides and show actual photos of places he had explored and the visual evidence of ancient truths that have remained hidden to many of us.

Frank Joseph is by nature a curious investigator and truth seeker. He has authored many eye-opening books on ancient mysteries, addressing everything from Atlantis and the Ark of the Covenant to Lemuria and the lost treasure of King Juba. For seventeen years after its inception in 1993, he served as the editor in chief of *Ancient American,* a popular archaeology magazine.

I recall Frank's early fascination with the hand-painted rune stones that our acquisitions editor, Nancy Mostad, gave him years ago to spark his interest in his own roots. That really hooked him. His investigation of the origins, significance, and power of the runes might surprise you.

You see, the runes are much older than most people commonly believe; and they are more widespread in their influence around the world than is commonly recognized. The runes date back to the Stone

Age in Europe and are probably the oldest written European language. "The English word *write*," according to Thorolf Wardle, among the most influential rune masters of modern times, "comes from the Anglo-Saxon *writan*, which first meant to 'carve' or 'score.' *Writan* is akin to German *ritze* ("score," "carve") and Scandinavian *rita/rista*. Hence, English *write* betokens the skill of carving runes into wood, stone, and so forth—runecraft!"[1] The runes represent the ancient gods and goddesses as expressions of cosmic energies, which the Christian church sought to suppress.

What commonly survived, then, of this ancient folk tradition was a watered-down version presented as little more than superstition. The glyphs and the power inherent in their descriptions are much more than that, however. They contain our oldest myths and earliest archetypes.

Frank Joseph's *Gods of the Runes,* so magically illustrated by the British artist Ian Daniels, makes the ideograms come to life for you with the original names, meanings, stories, and castings to capture the ritual power in your own reading of the runes.

VON BRASCHLER,
MINNEAPOLIS ORGANIZER OF THE THEOSOPHICAL SOCIETY
AND AUTHOR OF *A MAGICAL JOURNAL*

Connecting with the God Energy of the Runes

When we see runes today, they still affect us, as they affected the ancient Northmen with a sense of mystery and primitive power.

ROBERT HIXSON,
"RUNES WHISPER FROM THE PAST," *FATE*

There are many books about the ancient runes and their role in personal divination. Yet modern practitioners miss out on the real basis of their power. Old Norse words associated with these glyphs have become more cerebral than mystical. Not so the original runic magic.

Current labels used for each sign are relative latecomers that replaced the signs' previous names in the mid-thirteenth century, when the church sought to demonize all forms of pre-Christian spirituality. "The Christianizers of the sixth and seventh centuries," wrote Thorolf Wardle, "altered the rune names to falsify the holy heathen bequest."[1] The runes were originally intended as symbols for specific deities whose particular kind of divine energy might be accessed. In other words, every rune was identified with a specific immortal, the gods and goddesses of the Nordic world.

Gods of the Runes is unique among all other books available on the subject, because it discards the watered-down, postpagan nomenclature still in use, and instead employs the original version, identifying each rune with the deity it was meant to signify. We benefit from this inceptive association, because the runes become personalized in the eternal figures of myth. The runes thus offer an otherwise lost sense of identification with the cosmic energies that inspired Norse divination, while providing a more profound and meaningful interpretation than is available from conventional systems.

In *Gods of the Runes,* each of the twenty-four ideograms is associated with a specific god or goddess—and the deities are introduced through their own legends to exemplify each rune and illustrate the god's or goddess's relation to it. Included are the mythic figure's astrological period, identifying color, and gemstone. The rune's positive and negative qualities are then described in the context of its divine patron. In a final chapter, readers become acquainted with ancient spreads used by Norse adepts for character and situation analysis and divination. They discover where and when the runes were conceived—at a time and place radically removed from our present understanding of their provenance.

Runes were and still are elements of ritual. As defined by the great American mythologist Joseph Campbell, a ritual is the reenactment of a myth, and myths are the collective dreams by which a preliterate people preserve the truths most important to them.[2] A similar conclusion was ascertained a century earlier by another extraordinary scholar— Guido von List, who perceived the runes as ceremonial links to myth: "According to the rule of mysticism, every magical belief moves parallel to mythology, in that the mythic pattern is adopted in analogies to human-earthly processes, in order to reach results similar to those given in the myths."[3] Runes are, therefore, perennial archetypes of formative psychic energies recognized many thousands of years ago, but still alive, if dormant, in the modern mind.

In stripping away the veneer of confusing complexity that has accreted on the subject for the past eight centuries, the runes reappear in their pristine simplicity, just as they were meant for everyday use by ordinary men and women. No longer the esoteric property of self-styled rune masters, they are here restored to their original function as a popular means of connecting with potent psycho-spiritual forces within and outside ourselves. *Gods of the Runes* is the most authentic and, therefore, effective version of Old Norse divination—the rediscovery of runic origins, the runes' dormant powers, and their modern relevance.

Rune Quest
Exploring Methods of Divination

A rune is literally a mystery containing the secrets of the inner structure of existence. Every character that we call a rune is a storehouse of knowledge and meaning.

NIGEL PENNICK,
THE COMPLETE ILLUSTRATED GUIDE TO RUNES

In 1993, I was painting a cat. Actually, it was the plaster cast of an Egyptian statue representing Bastet, the cat goddess of pleasure. Painting casts of ancient artifacts was my hobby at the time, but this latest project was something special. It was intended as a gift of appreciation to a valued friend. Nancy Mostad, the acquisitions editor at Llewellyn Worldwide, a Saint Paul, Minnesota, company, had been instrumental in the publication of my first book, *Sacred Sites: A Guide to Sacred Centers and Mysterious Places in the United States,* the previous year.

Aware of her devotion to both the goddess in particular and cats in general, I wanted to surprise her with the two-foot-tall Bastet statue. I spent some three weeks painstakingly completing the multicolored necklace, earring, stand, and other features. At last, I carefully installed its glass eyes, which gave the figure a startlingly lifelike appearance. Bastet was carefully loaded in the front seat of my car, and we drove

Fig. 1.1. Bastet as the white cat

from my home near Chicago to Lakeville, a Saint Paul suburb, where Nancy and I planned to have dinner with a mutual friend. Before the table was set, I placed in front of her the tall object, veiled by a cloth. Nancy had an active sense of the mysterious, and I enjoyed conducting minor melodramatic exercises such as this one. After completing some overblown narration about "the living deities of ancient Egypt," I whisked off the concealing cloth to reveal the proud, bejeweled, sacred white cat goddess in all her painted, plaster glory.

Nancy was dumbstruck, perhaps for the first time in the life of this otherwise formidable young woman. I beamed with pride, sure that she had been profoundly moved by the wholly unexpected expression of gratitude for her efforts on my behalf. That, however, was only partly the cause of her speechless amazement. Her only response was to hand me a small, cloth bag. It was tied and covered with abstract patterns that were vaguely reminiscent of traditional folkish designs from northern Europe. I undid the knotted string. Inside the bag was a collection of pebbles, individually different, yet generally similar in size, and all apparently water-worn. Each one was emblazoned with a Norse rune, skillfully painted blood red.

Unbeknownst to me, for the previous three years, whenever Nancy visited (in her case, "made a pilgrimage to" would be closer to the truth) a sacred site on what she referred to as the North Shore—somewhere along the Minnesota coast of Lake Superior—she carefully selected a particular kind of rock that she needed to make her rune stones. After she collected the proper number, she hand-painted all twenty-four, then sewed a bag for them. She had only recently completed her project, and she chose my Lakeville visit as an opportunity to present it. Unaware of our separate labors, we had worked simultaneously to create sacred objects for one another, and independently decided to give them to each other at the same time. Our meaningful coincidence added a mystical dimension to the exchange of statue and runes that substantially enhanced their personal significance. Also, Mardal-Freya, the Norse goddess of love and divine keeper of the sacred mysteries, is symbolized by a pair of white cats (see the front cover of this book). I could not have hoped for a more magical introduction to the occult practices of the Vikings, their ancestors, and their descendants.

Some years before this most appropriate encounter, I was developing a growing fascination for divination and its kindred phenomenon: synchronicity. This latter twist of the paranormal was also the title of a book by Carl Gustav Jung, the man who coined the term.[1] He wrote at length about an ancient Chinese prognosticating system, the I Ching, or Book of Changes, which was founded on the belief that humanity and the cosmos share the same life energies and are more closely interrelated than external appearances suggested. An individual human being and blade of grass are linked in an all-encompassing matrix that is more experienced than seen. The identical motions of an infant spiraling out of its mother's womb or a galaxy spiraling and swirling around a black hole in outer space respond to the common rhythms of nature. Determining the patterns of one must reveal those of another.

To trace the outlines of that subtle link that connects the visible and invisible nexus between the microcosm of humankind and the macrocosm of the universe, the I Ching is composed of sixty-four symbolic hexagrams. Each hexagram comprises two three-line *pa kua,* or trigrams. The eight basic trigrams, each with its own name and meaning, are stacked one above the other in various combinations to form the sixty-four hexagrams. Line by line, the individual hexagrams are built up from the bottom by successively casting lots. Solid and broken lines signify the cosmic male and female principles, respectively. The interaction of this yin-yang duality, as the fundamental creative power, explains all coming changes that the individual diviner casts by lot.

The I Ching is very old—it is said to have been discovered by the legendary emperor Fu Hsi in the twenty-fourth century BC, when he noticed the hexagram pattern on the shell of a tortoise emerging from the Yellow River after a destructive flood. The earliest archaeological evidence of the I Ching were oracle bones from the Shang dynasty, circa 1500 BC. Three hundred years later, the I Ching's first known practitioner, Wen Wang, is believed to have invented the prognosticating hexagrams. Any divination method able to operate in continuous use for the past three or four millennia has certainly stood the test of time for millions of modern-day practitioners.

Though obviously part of a sophisticated system, the I Ching was nevertheless based on superstition, I had always assumed. I was all the more surprised, then, when I read of Jung's high regard for classic Chinese divination. The most important pioneer of modern psychology in the twentieth century used his long-term investigation of Fu Hsi's hexagrams as the basis for *Synchronicity,* because, the Swiss scholar insisted, they worked.[2] He reported that in randomly throwing the coins (originally, dry yarrow stalks), they often fell into logical patterns that corresponded to current circumstances or psychological conditions, and they accurately foretold coming events in the life of an individual diviner. Jung's emphasis, of course, was on a subconscious relationship between coincidental arrangements of inanimate objects (the I Ching coins) and their perceived meaning to the person casting the hexagrams. Such is the stuff of synchronicity.

Though I was reservedly open to the possibilities of Jung's discussion, I was nonetheless intrigued enough to pursue my own research through an appropriate divination vehicle. I tried duplicating his alleged success with the I Ching, but it struck no sympathetic chord with me, and my results were negligible. Friends urged me not to despair, however. They argued that everyone had to find a method suited to his or her individual personality. From the broad variety of fundamentally similar tarot decks available, the Mythic Tarot, which uses images from Greek mythology, was suggested, considering my interest in such legendary material.[3]

I studied and practiced with the cards, eventually attaining some degree of competence over time. Not infrequently, they did indeed reflect the current condition of my life and correctly foretold events in the immediate future. I usually consulted them before traveling, only to discover that the cards often indicated circumstances beyond the possible realization of any subconscious wish-fulfillment. Previous to one such overseas' journey, the cards informed me that I would undergo a sense of profound loss in the Canary Islands. They refused to be more specific, but urged me to go on the trip in any case. Some three months later, having just stepped off my ship onto the Canary Island of Tenerife, I realized that I had left in my cabin an item of significant personal value. All search efforts to find the object were in vain, and only after experiencing the pain of its disappearance did I recall that the tarot reading had accurately predicted my situation.

At such moments, the persuasion of rational explanations deteriorated before a growing impression, formed by so many similar experiences, that the deck had to be operating on a level other than that of mundane cause and effect. Prevailing logic to the contrary, Jung's suspicions seemed to me confirmed: some unseen yet demonstrable connection between the apparently unrelated elements of mere cards and future events existed after all.

Although too many examples of the tarot's accuracy argued convincingly for its validity, I began to feel uncomfortable with the system. Despite a deepening respect for its undeniable efficacy, I gradually withdrew from using it. A negative, nameless uncertainty generated by the deck made me shrink from a kind of dank, unfamiliar darkness that I perceived about its corners, with the tarot's unsettling images of the Hanged Man, Death, and the Devil. To be sure, the cards allowed a competent practitioner to see far—perhaps too far—into the future. But I could not escape the same sort of revulsion described by Joe Fisher, who eventually killed himself after dabbling too deeply in mediumship: "No matter how hard I tried, I could not shrug off a cloying sense of contamination which could neither be pinpointed nor explained."[4] Learning that others had reacted with a similarly nonspecific dread of the tarot, I finally put the deck aside.

Divination appeared to be real, if immoral, in a way beyond what my conscious mind could grasp, let alone explain. Yet the phenomenon pursued me. My sister Chris, who was unaware that I had given up on such forms of prophecy as indefinably icky, presented me with a new deck as a birthday gift. The animal Medicine Cards were altogether different from the spooky tarot, however.[5] They featured the attractive images of deer and otter, butterflies and swans, hummingbirds and horses—forty-four creatures in all, each one associated with its own psycho-spiritual inflection. These natural archetypes were not so powerfully efficacious as their darker counterparts in the Major and Minor Arcana, but they were more, as Chris described them, user-friendly. For all their affability, however, the animal Medicine Cards seemed to lack range or depth. Moreover, they sprang from a Native American tribal view with which I could never personally identify, however much it merited admiration and respect.

The deck was a modern contrivance in which its well-intentioned creators endeavored to distill in written words and representational art the various traditions of a preliterate people who were uninterested in anything of the kind beyond simple petroglyphs. When I worked with the animal Medicine Cards, I sometimes felt like an outsider looking in on another, exclusive mind-set. I dreaded resembling a pathetic Indian wanna-be, like too many lost white Americans who looked for spiritual guidance, and I could not imagine a real tribal elder or shaman using them to achieve illumination.

Why, then, should anyone else, unless the deck was meant to appeal to Pale Faces who did not know better? In the end, my disenchantment with the cards was completed by a deepening sense of cultural alienation. I was no more able to embrace them as an important part of personal guidance than a Native American conscious of his or her own spiritual background could be expected to follow the tarot. Giving me the mythic version of the tarot, featuring ancient Greek imagery, had been my friends' attempt to offer something with which I might more easily identify than the Chinese I Ching. Here, too, however, was the odor of inauthenticity and compromise. Acrylic renderings of the River Styx, Prometheus, and Pan tried to cover the original, underlying forms, but the grimmer outlines of Death, the Hanged Man, and the Devil always showed through the modern veneer.

Like the animal Medicine Cards, this tarot did not trace back to ancient origins, but instead was a modern contrivance. The tarot is, however, steeped in a very old and powerful esoteric tradition unsuspected by many of its practitioners—namely, the quest for the Holy Grail. A comparison of symbolic content readily demonstrates that the cards illustrate Wolfram von Eschenbach's medieval story *Parsifal:* the Fool meets the same characters in the Major Arcana—a Magician (Klingsor) and a Fisher King and the Queen of Zazamanc (the deck's Emperor and Empress). He becomes one of the Lovers seeking Justice through Temperance—likewise names for various tarot cards. The first suite in the Minor Arcana, the Suite of Cups, is a fourteen-card representation of the sacred Grail itself. In the beginning of Wolfram's epic, Parsifal is equivalent to the Page of Cups, later becoming the Knight of Cups who encounters the Grail lady, Repanse de Schoye, the Queen of Cups. Gawain's vision in the Grail of Christ crucified appears as the

Hanged Man, while Amfortas, the king of Monsalvat, the Grail castle, is a true King of Cups.

The Grail romances, beginning with Chretien de Troyes' version around AD 1175, were mostly composed from the late twelfth to fifteenth centuries.[6] Their popularity continued throughout western Europe into the early 1400s, when the tarot was invented as a kind of underground device to preserve and promote the Grail quest's non-Christian spirituality, rightly suspected as heretical by church authorities. Modern commentators Helen Mustard and Charles Passage point out that "the Grail of the romances is found in a castle, not in a church; a king, not a priest, is its keeper; a female carries it, contrary to all church usages relative to the Eucharist; the Holy Grail does not appear in literature or in art prior to Chretien's time; nor did the Church ever recognize the Holy Grail as a valid Christian relic."[7] Prelates were particularly disturbed by the tarot's thematic resemblance to the proscribed ideology of the Knights Templars, long associated with the Grail. Not coincidentally, *Parsifal* had been composed at a time when the order was in full career. Wolfram himself hints in Book 1 that he was a knight of the Templars, whose esoteric principles he thinly shrouded in fiction.

Despite its appealing origins in the Grail romances, the tarot, like the animal Medicine Cards and the Chinese I Ching (which was at least culturally authentic), seemed to me too alien for personal use. Joseph Campbell had cautioned Westerners to look for spiritual clues in their own European background, and I was already considering the Norse runes in this context when Nancy Mostad presented them to me. Unlike the previous systems I investigated, something inside me resonated instantly and positively to their sight and touch. Her kindness in personally making them for me and the magic of the meaningful coincidence that brought them into my possession combined with at least some previous knowledge of the ideograms to make them uniquely appealing. I was already familiar with the Elder Futhark, as the twenty-four characters are known for their first six runes (the *th* is formed by a single glyph).

Thirty years before, while I was still a teenager, I visited a rare-book store and had been fortunate enough to find the elegant, cloth-bound, twin volumes (one in burgundy; the other, scarlet) of *The Viking Age,* which describes the runic script in detail.[8] Paul Du Chailu's late-nineteenth-century classic became one of my favorite books. Thanks to him, I scribbled runes all over my high school notebooks and anything else that seemed suitable. Observing my runic passion, a friend gave me a replica of a Viking ax, the long handle of which I immediately inscribed with such appropriate statements as, "May the will that wields me be as strong as my steel," "Ask my name—It is Skull Splitter," and "Die handling me against your enemies and see the Aesir [the Norse gods]." Clearly, the runes still had a power to evoke in me strong imagery—and they seemed to me to have an indefinable magical quality all their own.

When Nancy gave me the set she made, however, I knew little of their role in divination; I consulted all available volumes of instruction that told how the runes were to be properly read. These texts were written by leading modern authorities, but I did not neglect several earlier sources. Every rune master or rune mistress added his or her own inflection on the study, but it was satisfying to learn that they all conformed to a general uniformity of interpretation, which imparted a fundamental validity to the system each described. I felt far more comfortable with the runes than any other divination method, and I achieved if not spectacular results, then at least some small measure of gratifying success through following their practice. Yet even they made me feel uneasy in a way I did not understand, although to a far lesser degree than the tarot or animal Medicine Cards. There was something unfulfilled or incomplete about the runes; almost as though they were somehow off-kilter. I was reacting with an instinctive knowledge that my rational mind could not comprehend.

Re-reading and expanding my rune library or consulting with rune-ologists failed to dispel this persistent disquiet. I nevertheless continued to use the runes in the hope that some level of growing competency would eventually overcome my nameless angst. Events, however, moved me down a less logical path that would lead to the root of my runic discomfort and beyond to a wonderful revelation about the runes, their real origins, and ultimate purpose. That path opened up while I made plans to visit western Europe and North Africa as part of my research for a book I was writing about Atlantis.[9] I wanted to collect local traditions that described the lost civilization and the Great Flood alleged to have destroyed it. In Scandinavia, rural folklore was said to still preserve ancient memories of a primordial cataclysm, the Ragnarok, or the Breaking of the Gods, with its Atlantean overtones of a former age of greatness that sank beneath the waves and ruined palaces that came to rest on the ocean floor.

The runes were far from my conscious mind, however, as I prepared for an exciting quest overseas. In the process of forming an itinerary, though, a name began circulating through my thoughts. Unsummoned, it repeated itself over and over in my mind, like the refrain of an annoying melody caught in an endless loop: "Roskilde, Roskilde, Roskilde." I guessed it was somewhere in Denmark, but that was all. Still, for almost a week, its name continued to circle around my waking hours like a pesky insect, until I finally did some reading about Roskilde.

I learned that a Viking ruler, Hroar, founded his capital there, in eastern Zealand, near a number of sacred springs, or *kilde,* in the early eleventh century. It remained the seat of Danish monarchies for the next four hundred years. Contemporary with Hroar were several sailing vessels, including a magnificent long-ship found almost perfectly preserved near the head of the Roskilde Fjord during the mid-twentieth century. A large museum displaying the thoroughly restored flotilla was opened to the public in 1969. While none of this may have had anything to do with runes or Atlantis, I determined to go to Roskilde, if only to satisfy an abiding interest in Viking culture and to learn why (if any cause existed) the inexplicable repetition of its name apparently urged me to visit the place.

I arrived in Bergen, Norway, from Aberdeen, by Scottish ferryboat, then I traveled south to Kristiansand. Another ferry took me to the northernmost tip of Denmark, at Skagen, from which I explored the rest of the country, including Roskilde, just outside Copenhagen. Half expecting some profound revelation as I disembarked from the local train, I was not disappointed by the Viking Ship Museum's one-hundred-twenty-foot vessel. It was hard to believe that its nearly pristine timbers, so gracefully curved into the capacious hull and exquisitely fashioned into bow and stern posts, were a thousand years old. Whatever blast of spiritual illumination I anticipated was obscured by awe of the splendid woodcarvers' genius and maritime technology fused into this medieval masterpiece. Here, indeed, was the harmonious blending of art and science from which our culture could still learn much.

Yet Roskilde did, after all, provide a revelation that disclosed secrets about the runes that I could not find in any book. Visitors to the Viking Ship Museum naturally focus on the star attraction for which it is named, but they often overlook the hundreds of other, less dramatic Viking age relics on display in vacuum-sealed glass cases along the walls of the adjacent salons. In one of them, among the most ancient surviving examples of Futhark, is displayed a wooden staff or baton on which runes are inscribed. Its discovery at Roskilde seemed appropriate, given the antiquity of the city and its relatively close proximity to the Jutland Peninsula, where Denmark joins Germany—in the place where the mid-first-century-AD Meldorf brooch, the oldest known artifact with runic writing, was found. What made the Roskilde staff—older than the proud long ship by at least ten centuries—particularly interesting was the Norsemen's identification of its runes with their gods.

I experienced a flash of recognition, one of those "ah ha" moments when prolonged uncertainty and obdurate confusion are suddenly brushed aside by The Answer. All the disorganized blocks fell into place, creating a solid, recognizable edifice. I knew then the source of my disquiet with the runes. Additional research was needed to verify my strong suspicions, but I finally felt a spiritual bonding with Futhark that had been prevented by my modern misconceptions about the Nordic system.

All present-day runeologists assign the same individual names to each glyph. When I tried to learn the runes, I found, as most students do, that these appellations were not only unfamiliar but also difficult to associate with the ideograms. Fehu, Uruz, Thurisaz, and the rest meant nothing to me—or to Scandinavians or even Icelanders, who still speak Norse. As with the I Ching, tarot, and animal Medicine Cards, modern Western readers are culturally alienated by such foreign words and unable to connect on a fundamental level with the energies intended by the runes. I learned that these names are by no means ancient or original. At least half of them stem from the mid-seventeenth century. The rest go back no more than another five hundred years. They first came into being during the late twelfth century, after a Vatican decree of death was imposed on anyone caught using the runes. Unrepentant "heathens" who defied the pope learned, to their sorrow, that he was serious. Du Chaillu recounts the awful fate of a Viking chief, Olof, who fought for the spiritual independence of his people and lost to a coalition of Norwegian Christians.[10] Their bishop had the captured man fettered to a table while his mouth was forced open by a large, metal funnel into which venomous snakes where forced to crawl down his gullet by means of a burning torch inserted at the wide end of the funnel.

Despite demonic countermeasures such as these, courageous rune masters maintained their craft, albeit in underground circumstances. It was then that some of the words for the runes known today were invented to take the place of their original god titles. The runes' hold on northern European folkish consciousness was so strong, however, that they not only survived the Dark Ages but also regained such a high degree of popularity by 1639 that they were banned again by yet another papal decree. As before, new labels for the runes were made up to disguise any connection with the old gods. Together, the twelfth- and seventeenth-century inventions are those by which the runes are now known. In other words, labels for the ideograms used by present-day runeologists were devised only eight hundred and three hundred years ago as substitutions to disguise pre-Christian mythic associations during periods of severe religious repression. They are not their authentic names.

Originally, each rune was meant to be associated with a specific deity. Some of this inceptive intent still survives in at least one rune: Tyr, also known as Tiwaz, probably because his spear-shaped glyph was self-evidently that of the Germanic war god. Identifying each rune with its correct mythic figure did not seem feasible, however. Such knowledge, which was probably never documented in writing but preserved only through oral tradition, had been deliberately effaced with the substitution of code words that came to make up Futhark as it is still understood today. Moreover, the Norse and their Old European predecessors worshipped a vast pantheon of deities, many of whom fell in and out of favor over time or were absorbed by immortals that were similar to them. Reverence for some endured for countless generations, while others, once widely honored, vanished, leaving behind not even their names.

Two factors made restoration of the runic gods possible. For all the centuries of church persecution and modern misinterpretation, the esoteric meaning behind each rune still survives intact. So enduring is the power of folk wisdom that eight hundred years of ecclesiastical propaganda and terrorism were unable to expunge it. An investigator had only to match the runes' individual characteristics and qualities with those of the old gods to determine those that belonged together. While the Norse did indeed know a vast number of deities, many of them lost to history, they consistently venerated twenty-four mythic figures that often changed names over time but retained a fundamental similarity of type—essentially as Egypt's Thoth became the biblical Enoch, or the Greek Zeus donned Roman garb to become Jupiter. Once we become familiar with the mythology known to the rune makers of old, it becomes clear that they continuously honored the same twenty-four deities—under occasionally different names. They divided them into three categories: six Aesir (gods), six Asynir (goddesses), and twelve Vanir (gods and goddesses). We need only match their attributes to those of the runes to determine which rune represents a specific deity.

We immediately run into trouble with this interpretation, however. Some rune masters today insist on casting twenty-five ideograms, although the Norse—like all other peoples—never revered a twenty-five-member pantheon. The numeral is entirely improper in cosmological terms and is actually antithetical to the most basic creation system. As an odd number, it additionally sabotages any attempt at divination, which traditionally depends on the cyclical quality of even numbers to function properly. Having a twenty-fifth rune throws the entire method off balance. During my studies, I learned that the original number of runes corresponded to the twenty-four Aesir, Asynir, and Vanir, because they represented double the sacred cosmological number par excellence: twelve. This number signifies the cosmic order, the twelve houses of the zodiac, the twenty-four hours of the day, the twelve months of the solar year, the twelve pairs of ribs in the human body, the twelve thoracic vertebrae in the human spine, and so forth.

The runic system was very anciently a zodiac wherein its twenty-four glyphs symbolized deities representing different astrological houses. Modern investigators could undertake the reconstruction of this double zodiac, associating each god or goddess with his or her own proper place in a long-lost Wheel of Life—and their success may be gauged by the accuracy of its forecasts. In any case, remnants of this prehistoric Norse zodiac still existed in "the Scandinavian calendar staff, which down to the previous century, preserved runes as time-designators," according to runic scholar Karl Theodor Weigel in 1935. He concludes that "these symbols [were] clearly taken from the course of the seasons."[11] The runes' relationship to the sky—in an astrological or calendrical function, or both simultaneously—appears to have been the original impetus from which the runes emerged, as suggested by their double-twelve ideograms. A trace of these celestial connections survives in the names we still use for the days of the week. Each one was dedicated to a Norse god or goddess: Sunday from the solar deity, Sol; Monday from Mani, the moon goddess; Tuesday from Tyr (or Tui,

Tiwaz), god of war; Wednesday from Wotan (Wodan, Odin), chief of the pantheon; Thursday from Thor, the Thunderer; Friday from Frija, queen of the immortals; and Saturday from Syn, the divine patron of justice.

Twelve was revered as the most essentially important number throughout the ancient world, because it was seen as an expression of celestial recurrences and the organization of the universe itself. Each god and goddess presided over an hour of the day, necessitating twenty-four divinities. They thus became personifications of the cosmic order that governed all creation in the orderly revolution of time. It was fundamentally imperative, therefore, that any system presuming to establish for its practitioners a rapport with the spiritual energies of the cosmos must rest on a duodenal framework or its multiple. That the Norse chose to work through a divination method that was twice twelve demonstrates their respect for its primary significance as the cosmological number. For them, all numerals innately possessed a dual character: They were simultaneously mundane (utilitarian) and sacred (when they corresponded to unseen forces of the mind, soul, and god energy). It was because of numbers' spiritual implications that twenty-four runes were deliberately chosen not only to reflect but also interact with the cosmic order.

In 1985 a respected author of the paranormal, Murray Hope, concluded, "After several years of experimenting, I settled for the twenty-four basic runes and added one blank to represent fate or karma, making a total of twenty-five. Five is Odin's sacred number and five times five equals twenty-five, which resolves into the psychic number seven. My magical workings are based on this system."[12] In other words, runic divination was appropriated to suit Hope's new method. In all other cosmological traditions, seven is never a psychic number and is invariably associated with the sun and the completion of cycles of time: the seven days of the week, the seven major chakras, the seven colors of the rainbow, and so forth.

Hope believed five was "Odin's sacred number," unlike the Norse, who identified their supreme goddess, Frija, the queen of heaven, with nine, the numeral of creation. Nine is always the result if it is multiplied by itself or any other single numeral, and then the two numerals produced are added together. For example, $9 \times 9 = 81$ $(8 + 1 = 9)$; $7 \times 9 = 63$ $(6 + 3 = 9)$; $3 \times 9 = 27$ $(2 + 7 = 9)$, and so forth. The result of any sequential number subtracted by its reverse invariably results in nine: $54 - 45 = 9$; $65 - 56 = 9$; $21 - 12 = 9$, and so forth. These uniquely peculiar qualities underscore nine's mystic creativity, perpetually reproducing itself through innumerable couplings, resulting in the nine months of pregnancy. It is, therefore, the number of reproduction, renewal, and rebirth.

Since Murray Hope contrived a twenty-fifth blank face to make the runes conform to his own system of "magical workings," every set available to the public includes his self-styled fate rune. Present-day runeologists are to be complimented for their invaluable preservation of the meanings and often insightful interpretations of individual glyphs. Their work, however, is subverted by the modern addition of this bogus rune. Their efforts are further undermined by the use of twelfth- and seventeenth-century code words in place of the original god names with which readers may more easily and intimately identify—as intended.

Some writers with little understanding of and less empathy for genuine mysticism join these obstacles to authentic rune work with the practice—as deeply offensive as it is politically correct—of blurring Odin's identity with that of Jesus, or deliberately conflating Frija and the Blessed Mary, because both were, after all, referred to as "the Queen of Heaven."[13] Theirs is the same modus operandi wielded by Dark Age proselytizers to dilute indigenous spirituality—whether among northern Europeans or New World Native Americans—thereby obliterating it. The runes cannot be associated with Jesus, Buddha, Krishna, and so forth, because they predate these historical figures by thousands of years. More important, the runes provide entirely different messages than these later saviors offered. While modern syncretists may be so edified as to embrace all religions as interchangable—their apparent dissimilarities merely cultural inflections of no real significance—the same does not apply to the runes, because they connote the particular qualities of specific deities that made no pretense at universality. They were and are the unique manifestation of, by, and for a distinct mind-set as expressed in the deepest roots of western European mysticism.

Although the runes are today thus often misrepresented and abused, "they have nonetheless survived to the threshold of our time," Weigel assures us, "and manage, even now, to speak a clear language."[14]

For the Norse ideograms to speak as intended, however, they must be divested of their modern attachments, which distort the fundamental power and true spirit of the runes—with their ability to connect us to the psycho-spiritual energies that facilitate illumination. The oldest (original, authentic) rune series—Elder Futhark—comprised twenty-four ideograms that corresponded to as many gods and goddesses of the most ancient western European pantheon. As such, working with each individual rune was akin to praying directly to the particular god or goddess embodied in a specific glyph. I found that knowing something about the myths of the Aesir, Asynir, and Vanir made the runes come alive as they never could through the abstract, outdated code names invented for them during times of proscription and still used today.

Moreover, the deities' own stories or characters exemplify, simplify, and clarify the truths implicit in the runes, leading to a far more authentic experience. While studying the myths in depth, I began to perceive that they were not merely entertaining tales or even moralizing fables, but also poetic devices for conveying esoteric meanings. If, as Joseph Campbell believed, ritual is the enactment of myth, then working with the runes, which represent the gods, is just that: personal participation in re-creating the perennial stories and, through them, connecting to the spiritual truths that underpin the whole universe. Such truths have always showed through the colorful veils of myth—as long as viewers did not take the old legends at face value. They missed the point when they confused connotation for denotation (the dilemma, perhaps, of all major religions today). Literal interpretation of myth is superstition. Grasping what the myth implies is enlightenment.

Although a detailed knowledge of Norse mythology is by no means necessary for a successful rune reading, it is true nonetheless that the more familiar we become with the Aesir, Asynir, and Vanir, the more valuable the divination experience becomes, because the runes are their material symbols. Chapters 3 through 26 describe each deity and show how each reflects the qualities of the runes associated with his or her divine personality. Before we meet them, however, we must know from whence they came. How did they come into being, and what forces combined to create such dynamic entities?

From before the beginning of time there was Ginnungagap, the Chasm of Chasms, a void beyond dimension. Niflheim, an illimitable realm of mist and darkness, lay on one side. On the other spread a no less infinite region of blinding fire, Muspelheim. Over the course of unguessed eons, rivers from both regions spilled into Ginnungagap, filling it with an immeasurable sea of ice. From the frozen matrix a form began to emerge. This was Audhumla, a cow who kicked free of the ice and licked it for nourishment. Very gradually her tongue revealed two unimaginably enormous shapes. They belonged to the first giants, Ymir and his wife. Together they sired a race of titanic beings. *Sigmund's Edda* tells, "In earliest ages, when Ymir awoke, there was neither sea nor sand, neither Earth nor sky. All was chaos."[15]

Audhumla provided them nourishment until her licking of the ice produced a different, much smaller pair. These were the divine twins, Buri and Bestla. Ymir took an instant dislike to them, because he feared they would challenge his sole domination of all existence. He and his gigantic sons hunted them everywhere, intent on murder. Hiding in the cold darkness of Niflheim, Buri and Bestla gave birth to twelve children. Their eldest grandson was Odin. They taught him the secrets of the universe, which he vowed to some day use against their persecutors. When he came of age, Odin fashioned the first thunderbolt from one of his own thoughts, then hurled it at Ymir.

The giant's salty blood gushed out in a catastrophic deluge, drowning all his offspring and their mother, save Bergelmir and his wife, who fled to the remotest ends of creation, where they established a new kingdom, Jotenheim.

As the flood subsided into the oceans of the world, Odin and his siblings formed Midgard, humankind's home, from Ymir's body. His bones became hills and mountains. Huge boulders and smaller rocks were formed from his teeth. His hair and beard were turned in to every sort of plant and tree. His skull they fashioned into the vault of heaven, which floated with clouds made from the dead giant's brains. Numerous white and black maggots burrowed into his rotting flesh. The white maggots, because of their apparent tidiness, were transformed into little gardeners, elves responsible for tending all flowers, shrubs, and forests and given a magical kingdom of their own: Alfheim.

Their leaders evolved into another set of gods and goddesses, the Vanir. But the more rapacious black maggots were thrown in to Niflheim, where, evolving as ugly, little, misshapen dwarves, they became skilled miners, jewelers, and goldsmiths, lords of all subterranean wealth. Buri and Bestla now knew their busy children collectively as the Aesir, Creators of the Cosmos, who were henceforward revered as deities, although Aesir referred specifically to the gods, while the goddesses were more properly Asynir.

But Odin was not finished. He scooped his hand into the fires of Muspelheim, then flung the burning coals across eternity, where they continued in their regular courses as stars. Again from Muspelheim he hefted a great flaming stone and tossed it into the sky, where it hung suspended, radiating golden light and comforting warmth on Midgard. He then threw a massive chunk of ice from Niflheim to catch in the heavens as a lovely companion piece. For a time, both were motionless, and daylight seemed neverending. Odin imbued them with consciousness, and they became living deities, Sol and Mani. Bergelmir, however, sought revenge by dispatching two ravenous wolves to devour them. Ever since, the sun and moon flee around Midgard just ahead of Skoll and Hati, and they will do so until overtaken at Ragnarok, the end of the world.

Touring the wonderful beauty of Midgard, the Aesir debated what proper form the configuration of its inhabitants should take, when they came upon a pair of magnificent trees. These Odin formed into the first man and woman, Askr (the stalwart ash tree, provider of spear shafts) and Embla (the alder), from whom all human beings were descended.

Among their last acts of creation, the gods raised a cosmic tree, called Yggdrasil. Its roots were in Niflheim, Midgard encircled its middle bough, and Asgard rose among the upper branches. Here the Aesir built their heavenly kingdom of unparalleled palaces, halls, and vast estates from which they rule the universe—but not forever. The cyclical nature of being is to fulfill its destiny, then pass away, but return to begin the process again and again, throughout eternity. No one and nothing escapes as a prelude to rebirth. This is the meaning of Ragnarok—the tragic Breaking of the Gods, the Eternal Return, wherein life perpetually renews itself, a cosmic cycle of unseen patterns connecting us to the sacred mystery behind existence—the mystery that gives meaning to our destiny.

2

Runic Origins
Older than Suspected

*There arises for us the duty to rescue these symbols, to
collect them, so that their remnants are not lost precisely
just now in our time of folkish awakening.*

KARL THEODOR WEIGEL,
"WOHER STAMMEN DIE RUNEN?"

The contrived addition of a blank face to modern rune sets and continued use of long-outdated code words seriously hinders modern understanding of the Norse runes. Their appreciation is not helped by some
present-day runeologists and mainstream archaeologists who concur
that the runes were probably late-Gothic spin-offs from a northern Italic
language (possibly Etruscan), existing no earlier than the first century
BC. Yet a closer look at Futhark reveals that its roots are profoundly
deeper in time, with origins not in the Roman world but in a time long
before. In 1935, Weigel reports that "research has already found in some
courageous pioneers champions of the idea that actually far older rune
inscriptions exist than one previously wanted to admit."[1] Although his-
torians continue to debate runic beginnings, why should we concern
ourselves with the controversy?

First, accepting conventional explanations for the origin of the runes
cuts us off from a valid, esoteric heritage that has persisted for millen-

Fig. 2.1. A Viking rune master in pre-Columbian North America as depicted in this mural at the Rune Stone Museum, Alexandria, Minnesota

nia, not centuries. The endurace of this inheritance from the depths of prehistory into our modern era testifies to the resilient, indomitable potency of these strange symbols. More important, tracing their roots brings to light a latent, numinous power for the enhancement and enrichment of our own spiritual encounter with the runes

As we saw in chapter 1, Futhark is composed of phonetic symbols that belong to an all-purpose alphabet with commemorative, recording, identifying, and magical purposes. Medieval runes have been found from Iceland and Greenland to the Isle of Man, Athens, and the Black Sea. Some were carved into the floor of Istanbul's Hagia Sophia cathedral by less than reverant Norse visitors in the tenth century. About a dozen other runes, far more controversial, appear in North America. Foremost among these is the Kensington Runestone, a long inscription that recounts the late-fourteenth-century voyage of Christian Vikings to Minnesota, and Oklahoma's Heavener Runestone, emblazoned with

Fig. 2.2. Two views of the Kensington Runestone

a single name: Gnomedal, possibly Valley of the Gnomes, perhaps a dep-recatory reference to local tribal Indians a thousand years ago.

Scholars have identified approximately five hundred runes in Denmark, compared to an estimated seven hundred fifty in Norway. Sweden has the largest collection, with approximately three thousand examples. More than a thousand runes may be found in the province of Uppland alone. Virtually all these inscriptions date from the late-eighth to the mid-thirteenth centuries, mostly commemorating the deeds and deaths of royalty.

To be sure, Futhark suffered modifications under the influence of events in northwestern Italy during the early centuries BC. As the Etruscans were pushed out of dominance by Rome, some fled north into Germany, where they came into contact with the Goths. The names by which the runes are known today—*fehu* (originally *faihu*), *thuri-saz (thauris), wunjo (winja),* and so forth—are all Gothic words. They competently date Futhark to Rome's early imperial period. Over the following centuries it remained fundamentally unchanged but under-went local inflections with the reconfiguration of various runes. At the beginning of the Viking age, circa AD 800, the Norse were in posses-sion of what is now known as the Elder Futhark, certainly the most consistently authentic version available today. Subsequent developments, with the growing influence of Christianity, placed greater emphasis on recording historical events and people at the expense of divination. These later sets included the Anglo-Saxon and Northumbrian runes: the Younger Futhark. Gothic and medieval versions represented a final evolution before the rune practices were outlawed under pain of death.

They were revived during the late-nineteenth century by the single most influential runeologist, Austria's Guido von List. He rejected all known runic systems, suspecting they were distortions of an earlier, authentic, more magical method, part of an actual written language, the first ever used in Old Europe. During his efforts to distance the runes from their mundane function as recorders of vainglorious kings, he created an original arrangement based on eighteen spells found in the *Havamal*. The Words of the High One, a reference to All-Father Odin, the god of wisdom, was a collection of poetic maxims first penned sometime between the ninth and twelfth centuries, although obviously rooted in far older oral traditions. Von List's hope in devising his Armanen set was to recover the lost spiritual connotations of the runes, each one meant, as Pennick writes, to express "its magical relationship to the cosmos."[2]

The Armanen is the preferred runic system in present-day, German-speaking countries and many other nations besides, inferring that von List rightly defined a widespread yearning to contact some lost, spiritual authenticity implicit in the long-abused runes. His belief that they were vestiges of an Old European script predating even the first known written language in Mesopotamia represented an early suggestion among fellow investigators that the runes were originally individual, magical signs meant to express particular spiritual energies, and therefore they must have been invented long before the official appearance of Futhark less than two thousand years ago. In this regard, Weigel was on the cutting edge of research: "While [runic] inscriptions have been found in the south [the Italian Alpine region], the oldest runic monuments

Fig. 2.3. Guido von List

in the north [Sweden] are not to be understood as inscriptions in the usual sense. They have more the form of magical formulas . . . this older manner of usage shows us that the runes served quite special purposes; namely, cult purposes."[3]

These suspicions were not validated until the research of two outstanding mythologists in the last decades of the twentieth century. Marija Gimbutas, professor of European archaeology at the University of California, Los Angeles, and Mary Settegast, (University of California, Berkeley) independently concluded that repeated signs painted on cave walls during the Upper Paleolithic Age appeared to be runic.[4] While neither Gimbutas nor Settegast were sure these symbols actually belonged to a written language, comparisons made between the seventeen-thousand-year-old symbols and the Elder Futhark were unmistakable. They showed that eight were exact duplicates of the medieval runes.

These signs first appeared in southwestern Europe during the so-called Magdalenian Period, after a site found at La Madeleine, in the French Dordogne Valley. It was a time of unsurpassed art and mysticism, when the impressive cave paintings at Lascaux, Pair-non-Pair, Teyjat, Les Trois Freres, and sixty-four other known locations were executed. These images did not depict primitive hunting scenes, but instead formed a tableau dramatizing the rituals of a mystery cult that put initiates in accord with unseen spiritual forces driving natural phenomena. This cult spread across central Europe deep into Russia, but subterranean illustration was confined to a region between the Atlantic Ocean and the Rhône River. The dynamic realism with which horses, oxen, cows, aurochs, elk, and other ungulates were portrayed has never been equaled, attesting to a sophisticated mentality at odds with modern misconceptions of brutish cavemen. Caricatures of the Magdalenians as nomadic hunter-gatherers are contradicted by contemporary engravings from St. Michel d'Arudy, the Grotte de Marsoulas, and La Marche, which show that these people tamed the horse ten thousand years before other peoples were supposed to have pioneered the same domestication in the Near East.

The American encyclopedist William R. Corliss points out that the application of horse power "like that of cattle, was a key check-point in the efflorescence of civilization. This transition away from hunting-and-gathering is said to have occurred along with the beginning of agriculture about eight-thousand years ago in the Old World."[5] He goes on to describe the 1911 discovery of thirty-thousand-year-old beveled horse teeth at a Paleolithic site in France.

> When a modern horse is seen to have beveled front teeth, it is confidently assumed that this dental deformity is the consequence of "crib-biting"; that is, the chewing of wood railings, ropes, or even stone. Horses are theorized to do this when they are bored [i.e., stressed], and it is further supposed that *only* domesticated horses become bored. It follows then that beveled horse teeth, even if of great age, must have come from domesticated horses. Wild horses were obviously too busy trying to survive to be bored and gnaw on non-food items![6]

As such, the obvious implications of the Stone Age engravings at St. Michel d'Arudy, the Grotte de Marsoulas, and La Marche are supported by much older physical evidence for the domestication of the horse not only during Magdalenian times but also many thousands of years before. With the passing of the great cave artists, horse power was lost until its rediscovery in the Near East eight thousand years ago. It is in this far earlier epoch of human cultural richness that the runes are rooted. These glyphs are the first written expressions of concepts still viable after 170 centuries. They embody spiritual influences that transcend time through their reflection of the human condition, which has not fundamentally changed since man became *Homo sapiens sapiens*. The unbroken thread of that Upper Paleolithic connection to the runes is found in Lascaux's famous shaft painting. It depicts a stick man with erect phallus sprawled between a rhinoceros, who appears to be departing the scene, and a bison, entrails spilling prodigiously from its genital area. Near the stricken stick man is the image of a bird surmounting a stick as a kind of *baton de comman-dant*, or scepter.

Settegast points out that this shaft painting perfectly illustrates the cosmological myth from a Zoroastrian scripture known as the Bundahisn.[7] Although composed as late as the ninth century AD, it preserves an account of creation and the nature of the universe based on much older, pre-Persian material. The oldest Iranian version tells of Yima, the earliest king, and a primordial bull, who lived happily together until evil appeared for the first time, killing them both. From the body of the bull gushed forth marrow and semen to create the cosmos and the animal kingdom. Yima's body transformed into all the metals of the earth; his seed engendered humanity. Among Upper Paleolithic rock art in Europe and Africa, the rhinoceros embodied the principle of evil. Hence, its depiction at Lascaux, where it appears to have gored the bison (its entrails spilling out) and slain the ithyphallic stick figure, mirrors the Bundahisn creation myth. Yima lost his command of *xvarenah,* or the "kingly glory" (immortality), in the form of a bird, as depicted in the bird-headed scepter laying beside the stick man illustrated at Lascaux.

Remarkable as the survival of this seventeen-thousand-year-old story in Iranian tradition may be, its preservation in Germanic myth implies that both spiritual ideas and contemporary runes or prerunic forms were inherited from Magdalenian times. Settegast mentions that the Persian Yima is more than philologically related to the Viking age Ymir, who likewise lived a timeless existence with a bovine companion until he was killed and his corpse formed the cosmos.[8] Nor was he the only Norse deity with Stone Age roots. Fourth-millennium-BC images of a thunder god, complete with Thor's hammer and power belt, have been found on stone stele at Baia de Cris, in Romanian Transylvania, Natalivka, and Kernosovka, in the Lower Dnieper, and other sites, mostly in southeastern Europe. Contemporary with these engravings was the appearance of the rune associated with Thor.

As the Magdalenian faded, more runes began to appear in a form that is still popular. About twelve thousand years ago artists of a spin-off culture known as the Azillian painted them on stone pebbles, just like those Nancy Mostad presented to me in 1993. As the Old Stone Age shifted into Neolithic times, knowledge and use of these rune forms was not lost. On the contrary, they grew to include more than half of the Elder Futhark. Core signs of the Old European script, in use from 5300 to 4300 BC, featured no less than seventeen identical ideograms or their variants. Most likely they were never used as part of a written language, but instead were regarded as magical and spiritual glyphs that symbolized the mystery cult of the caves. As Weigel observes, "the rune was not only a letter, rather simultaneously a symbol."[9]

It was probably much later, around the first century BC, that they additionally began to serve as part of an alphabet under Gothic influence. In other words, the alphabetical runes were adapted from much earlier, individual ideograms that may have had similar phonetic or word values. Gothic, Etruscan, Greek, and Latin—any one from which scholars claim the runes directly descended—use adaptations of ABC, and so on. Futhark does not, demonstrating its lack of relationship to them and firmly indicating evolution from a source for glyphs that originally belonged to no syllabary but instead stood alone as individual symbols or emblems.

They also survived the passing of Neolithic times, as evidenced by Late Stone Age/Early Bronze Age rock carvings known in Sweden, in Bohuslän, as *haellristningar*. It was during this abrupt cultural transition from Paleolithic to Bronze Age Europe that the final set of twenty-four runes came into being. How they were brought about is part and parcel of the continent's most radical revolution from a settled, agricultural, peaceful matriarchy of cave artists that had lasted fourteen thousand years or more to a migrating, cattle-herding, bellicose patriarchy of metalsmiths. But out of prolonged strife between two cultural opposites, a deep and lasting accord was eventually reached. The spiritual systems of both resident Old Europeans and newly arrived Aryans from the steppes of central Russia—the Caucasus, from whence these prehistoric Caucasians came—were combined, not merged, to create two, complementary sets of twelve-member gods and goddesses: the Aryan Aesir-Asynir and the Old European Vanir.

Reflecting the folkish souls of their patrons, the Aesir were war-like gods of conquest—such as Thor, the thunderer, and Odin, whose name indicates someone in a rage. By contrast, the indigenous European Vanir were mostly deities of peace and abundance, such as the goddess of spring, Ostara, and Erda, the Earth Mother. These personifications of psycho-spiritual energies are neither entirely Norse nor Germanic, but instead combinations with far older conceptions, representing a synthesis of Stone Age/Bronze Age/Viking age gods and goddesses, each one expressing a particular mythic inflection in his or her own rune. Thus, the twenty-four ideograms are the union of two, twelve-member pantheons resulting from the joining of two different peoples. The Norse themselves recounted that, at the beginning of time, the Aesir and Vanir fought each other for control of the world but decided upon cooperation as a wiser course. As Gimbutas writes, "The world of religious myth reflects social reality."[10]

She concludes that Freyr and Freya, as brother and sister Vanir of peace and love, "clearly stem from the Neolithic or even earlier."[11] In the Norse creation story, the Vanir are depicted as autochthonous, literally sprung from the soil, which is how the Upper Paleolithic Europeans must have seemed to both themselves and the invading Aryans. The same version told how Buri and Bestla, the first gods, came from the ice, just as the Old Europeans emerged from the last ice age. Thus, even the most deeply prehistoric memories may be preserved over many thousands of years through the medium of myth. The origins of the runes and the Norse deities they represent seem clearly rooted in the Upper Paleolithic, from which they descended through the Azillian pebble painters, Neolithic rock artists, and Bronze Age invaders to Etruscan intermediaries, Gothic modifiers, Scandinavian users of Futhark, and, ultimately, modern runeologists.

Few realize they are the inheritors of a spiritual tradition going back to the early Stone Age with its mystery cult of the cave. Weigel believed that

> the origin of the strange rune signs lies where the beginning of our race itself lies. We must seek it in such distant times, and finally put an end to the argument we still hear today, even from reputable scholars; namely, that the runes either spread from the Black Sea to the north, or came from the Alps as derivitive Etruscan script. But their origin remains what their name means: mystical whispering.[12]

During their seventeen-thousand-year development, the runes, like the myths themselves, continued to operate simultaneously on esoteric and exoteric levels. Perhaps nowhere is this functioning dichotomy better illustrated than in Yggdrasil, the World Tree, sometimes referred to in the sagas as the Tree of Life, which hints at its metaphysical quality. To common people, it was a cosmic ash that supported the universe, including Midgard, or human existence, and Asgard, the higher realm of the gods and goddesses. But to initiates of the old religion, the perennial philosophy, it was a poetic metaphor for that mystical dimension better known in our time as kundalini yoga. In essence, this is a spiritual discipline aimed at unleashing internal forces entwining the base of the human spine. As they rise through various centers of energy to the crown of the head, these *chakras,* or "whirling wheels," become agitated and generate extraordinary states of higher consciousness, connecting body and soul to the inner and outer worlds of being. Released from all forms of physical bondage, the practitioner is free from want and desire in a condition analogous to godhood.

Both the kundalini concept and imagery are embodied in Yggdrasil, which symbolizes the spinal column, that Tree of Life. Around its lowest root of Hel is coiled the Nidhoegg serpent, gnawing perpetually, just as the kundalini power gnaws continually, to free itself in higher realization. The levels rising above correspond remarkably well to the seven major chakras described in kundalini yoga. Svartalfheim, located at the root chakra, is chiefly concerned with matters of self-preservation and ego, just as the black elves of Niflheim were known for their gross materialism. Next is Muspelheim, the Land of Fire, appropriately associated with the sacral chakra of burning sexual passion. Jotenheim, headquarters of the giants who ever seek to displace the gods, is rightly paired with the navel chakra's ambition for power.

Midway between the three chakras below and three above is Midgard, the land of human beings, whose chief motivation, love, is the core energy of the heart chakra. Ascending into the throat chakra for self-expression and creativity are the Vanir of Vanaheim, where dwelled Kvasir, the divine artificer. Ljusalfheim is the brow chakra of awareness, because the light elves of this domain were renowned for their foresight. Asgard, the home of the gods, parallels the crown chakra of spiritual connectedness.

Although Yggdrasil held nine realms to the seven major chakras of Indian kundalini, the system used in Taoist Qi Gong and the Buddhist Ninjitsu kuji-kiri—both allegedly relying on methods older and more authentic—is ninefold. In any case, Hel, in the Norse arrangement, is simply a location for the kundalini serpent energy, Nidhoegg, and not a chakra, while Niflheim, the realm of ice and cold, may have been a variant of the root chakra at Svartalfheim. Yggdrasil's resemblance to the kundalini Tree of Life is reaffirmed in the eagle atop its uppermost branches. In the Hindu system, Garuda is an eagle likewise at the top of the Tree of Life, signifying spiritual liberation and victory over all lesser forms of human energy. The Norse eagle had the additional feature of a hawk perched over its eye to underscore the awareness of supreme enlightenment. Yggdrasil featured a rainbow bridge that connected Midgard, the realm of humankind, and Asgard, the abode of the gods. In kundalini yoga, the seven colors of the rainbow are equivalent to the seven major chakras and their corresponding hues—the same significance—with the additional hint that human beings, through the coordination of their prime energy centers, have a direct link to godhood.

With runic and mythic beginnings in Upper Paleolithic Europe, influences from India, the supposed home of kundalini yoga, become doubtful. Rather, the concept may have originated millennia earlier, in the high spirituality of the cave painters, expressed itself in Magdalenian culture, then was carried eastward into the steppes of central Russia, where the Aryans made their home. They adopted the Tree of Life spirituality and brought it with them when they invaded the Indus Valley during the early second millennium BC. Diffusion of the chakra system, then, may have been from west to east, not from Asia in the east to the west.

A treasured artifact from pre-Viking times is physical evidence of Scandinavian origins for this diffusion. The Gundestrup Cauldron is a Keltic ritual vessel made of solid silver displayed at Copenhagen's Nationalmuseet. Although dated only as far back as the first century BC, the Danish receptacle features embossed decoration with recognizable thematic roots in the Bronze Age, such as the boy-on-the-dolphin motif more familiar in Greece. There, this image was known as the Neriad, one of a hundred such companions belonging to Poseidon, the sea god, and signifying a mystical, intimate relationship between human and animal. But the central figure on the Gundestrup Cauldron is a man, eyes closed in meditation, sitting in the well-known lotus position that is commonly associated with Buddha and kundalini yoga.

In his left hand, he grasps a snake, symbolic of the moon or lunar energy. In his right, he holds a torque, a twisted gold neck adornment that is synonymous with the sun or solar influences. In other words, he balances the subconscious and the conscious mind, death-renewal and eternity. These contrasting though complementary powers are exemplified by the two antlers he wears on his head and the similarly adorned deer at his right hand that holds the torque of immortality. Each spring the deer sheds its antlers in bloody strips to renew them; hence, the creature is a parallel to the natural forces of regeneration. The man identifies with these forces by wearing the horned headdress of the deer that stands close by.

Resemblance of not only this Eastern-like human figure but also the

Fig. 2.4. The Gundestrup
Cauldron's Master of Animals

beasts around him to the famous Stone Age cave paintings of Dordogne is so close that scholars often refer to the man on the Gundestrup Cauldron as the Master of Animals—the same figure portrayed on the walls at Les Trois Freres eight thousand years before. The bridge from that deeply removed time to the onset of the Viking age appears among three male figures in an adjacent panel on the vessel. They are depicted blowing Lurs horns, which became a characteristic musical instrument of the Northmen.

Whatever the origins of kundalini yoga, its appearance in Norse myth implies a deep antiquity and correspondingly lofty spirituality still expressed in the runes. The word *rune*—synonymous with "mystery"— is lost in a prehistory that dates back to early Paleolithic times in which the runes were invented. The Indo-European root *ru-* signifies something mysterious or secret. *Rune* is related to the Gothic *runar* for "secret," but in Norse it indicates "secret knowledge." In Old Germanic, *runa* similarly stood for an "encoded secret."[13] These early meanings imply an esoteric wisdom that the runes were originally intended to convey to anyone who was open to their inherent magic. As the noted runeologist Garman Lord observes, "It behooves us to bear in mind that the runes and their lore were once alive, surrounded by a body of legend that has not yet entirely died. It further behooves us to listen to the echoes of that legend."[14]

It is clear, then, that the runes were invented to assist the personal attainment of inner illumination. Each glyph was part of a kundalini-like system designed to vitalize or awaken the spinal energy centers that drive personality and together comprise the human soul. Aware of their psychic potential, ancient practitioners claimed mastery over all manner of occult powers, including divination from the perspective of an altered, higher consciousness. Therefore, merely interpreting the runes to learn what the future offered was and is a spiritual experience that connects their readers to the mystical energies that interpenetrate all life and shape the destinies of individual men and women. The runes were holy because they allowed humans to establish direct guidance from and a dialog with the divine shapers of fate. As Weigel stresses, "Before the runes became script and hence somewhat profaned, they were signs of bonding with the power of fate, with divine working. They are the result of an early understanding of eternal life through Nature—of the mythic Dying and Becoming. They are, therefore, a sacred tradition for us."[15]

Runes acted and still act as visual clues, universal archetypes, linking consciousness to the inner and outer worlds of perceived and underlying reality. Only this powerfully fundamental connection made by the runes and their Stone Age predecessors can account for such an enduring hold on our fascination after more than seventeen thousand years.

The following twenty-four chapters introduce these mythic archetypes. In discerning an original relationship between symbol and deity, the full extent of their identity and purpose after centuries of suppression and obfuscation becomes clear. Their perennial truths and sacred energies thus stand revealed in the old tales and personality traits of the runic gods and goddesses.

3

Frija
The Queen of Heaven

There was once an obscure but virtuous tribe of peasants known as the Winniles. Their homeland lay in what has since become northern Italy, where they scratched out a meager existence from the flinty soil. Even so, they were content with the purity of their simple lives.

One day, however, they were threatened by a violent people that history remembers only too well, because they lived up to their name: the Vandals.

As the Winniles prepared to defend themselves against these dangerous barbarians, they prayed to Frija, the queen of heaven, for assistance. She ordinarily assumed the form of a tall, naturally dignified woman with long, golden hair (see color plate 1). She was impeccably dressed, wearing a flowing gown bound by gilt cinctures and clasps, and she wore golden sandals on her feet. To appear in such glory before mere mortals, however, would be too much for them to bear. So, through the auspices of their shaman, she told the Winniles that her husband, All-Father Odin, was encamped near the battlefield where the armies of the Winniles and the Vandals agreed to fight the next morning.

"Just after the sun rises," she counseled, "have your women approach Odin's tent. Be certain that their long hair, for which they are famous, is combed over their faces."

The Winniles deemed this advice extremely peculiar but agreed

39

to do as they were told, because they had faith in her goodness and believed she had their welfare at heart.

When Frija returned to Odin's tent, her husband was excited about the coming battle. He could hardly wait to see the action and was determined to grant victory to the Vandals, for whom he had big plans.

"But they have a bad reputation," Frija slyly told him. "Why not call them something else in the morning. Give them a new name by which they may be ever victorious."

He answered that her counsel was wise and promised that the first name he pronounced the next day would belong to an invincible people. Thus happily resolved, he set up his bed so that it faced westward, in the direction of the Vandals' bivouac. Evening fell. Odin drifted into a deep sleep and was soon lost in dreams of his world-conquering army.

Just then, Frija stealthily turned his bed, a four-poster on wheels, so that it now faced the east, away from the Vandals' encampment, while her husband, unconscious of the change in the direction of his bed, snored away. She patiently waited throughout the night until dawn, then flung back the tent flaps and loudly disturbed her husband's rest. "Odin, get up! See, your victorious warriors are coming!"

The cobwebs of sleep still clung to his drowsy mind as he squinted into the rising sun. In its nearly blinding radiance he could barely make out a host of figures slowly approaching through the morning mists. It was the Winniles women, their long hair combed down over their faces, just as Frija had bade them.

"Who are those long beards?" he asked groggily.

She exclaimed, "They are the victors of this day, because you have given them a new name, just as promised!"

Henceforth, the Winniles were known as the Long Beards, better remembered as the Lombards. They handily defeated the Vandals and stripped the vanquished foe of so much war booty that their hitherto impoverished realm was forever transformed into one of the richest jewels in the Italian crown: Lombardy. The Vandals disappeared from history, leaving behind only their name, still synonymous with willful, brainless destruction. When Odin was fully awake, he laughed heartily at the witty deception practiced on him by his wife, and he commended her for her manipulative skill.

Frija's story exemplifies her rune, which transfigures want and distress into deserved material reward. She gave her name to Friday, still the traditional pay day throughout the Western world. Friday and Frija's place in the Norse zodiac (Himinbjorg, the Cliffs of Heaven, from June 21 to July 20) were and are appropriate for weddings—hence, the June bride. Frija is also the divine patroness of expectant mothers or couples experiencing difficulty in having a child, as the following myth demonstrates.

The destitute realm of King Rerir was on the verge of extinction, particularly because his wife seemed unable to conceive, a barrenness reflected in consistent crop failures. Famine threatened, and everyone prayed to Frija for assistance, but without apparent response. One day, a withered hag appeared at court. She seemed somewhat demented but insisted on presenting a royal gift. The scoffing guards were in the process of turning her out when the queen ordered them to let her pass into the hall. "The value of a gift lies in the spirit with which it is given," she said, "not its price." The old woman humbly approached, dropped a common apple into Queen Rerir's lap, and departed without a word. Nine months to the day of her visit, the queen gave birth to a handsome son and heir. Even before then, however, her kingdom was alive with blooming prosperity. Queen and land were blessed with fertility. Of course, the strange old lady had been Frija in disguise.

Herein the importance of nine as the sacred number of the Norse is revealed. It is Frija's own numeral, signifying woman's goddess power in the nine months of pregnancy. Frija's color is red for the river of life accompanying childbirth, and her stone is green tourmaline to foster the energies of honestly begotten prosperity. Her earliest shrines were erected on a coastal strip of Europe running along the North Sea shores of the Netherlands, including Ostfriesland and Nordfriesland, in Germany. The name Friesland is derived from Frija. It is still renowned for its special breed of cattle. Interestingly, Frija's rune, the first sign in Futhark, means literally "cattle," and is synonymous with "wealth," just as is the first letter of the Gothic and Greek alphabets. This word parallel demonstrates the common origins of Indo-European peoples in deeply ancient prehistory, when wealth was primarily counted in livestock among the cattle-herding Aryan tribes. It is also an inflection on Audhumla, the primeval cow that first manifested material reality. According to the runeologist Horik Svensson, "The cow is a female symbol representing nourishment and continuity"—genuine abundance.[1] Anything more becomes self-indulgence, leading to softness and decay.

These mythic and philological themes complement the materialist implications of the Frija rune. It, like every Futhark glyph, has its positive and negative sides. There is nothing inherently evil in wealth, but it does demand balanced responsibility. When it begins to dominate our lives to the exclusion of human, ideological, or spiritual values, then the real value of prosperity is lost. If the means of wealth become its end, it degenerates into extravagance, and the true purpose of its presence in our life is devalued. In its upright position, the Frija rune indicates fruitfulness, just rewards, generosity, nourishment, personal wealth, solid finances, and the fulfillment of physical goals. Stressed is the attainment of earned rather than inherited income. As Goethe observes, "The capable man makes his own luck."[2] In the same spirit, Guido von List tells his followers to "generate your own luck and you will have it!" He believed that "only the fool mourns over decay" (the loss of transient worldly wealth).[3]

Although the Frija rune signifies material prosperity and gain, it more fundamentally affirms that we have the skills and diligence necessary to attain what we seek. The inverse of this warns of the loss of these things, the irretrievable disappearance of physical riches and continuing disappointment should the failed methods not be put aside in time. Svensson emphasizes that the Frija rune stands for material accomplishment even when opposition makes success seem doubtful.[4] Against all odds, rewards can be won, but less by chance than through our own hard work and good planning.

4

Ullr

The Glorious One

There was a time—a dark time—when Odin, Asgard's supreme lord, was banished by his fellow Aesir. For nine years heaven's gate was closed to him. Out of respect for his former greatness, he was allowed to appoint someone as temporary ruler, but only with the other gods' consent. They unanimously approved his choice, Ullr, who was well liked for his intelligent fair-mindedness and simple lifestyle. With no interest in power or riches, his chief passions were skiing and archery. Ullr, moreover, was only half immortal, born of the goddess Sif and Thor's beloved stepson. His divine mother had long before presented Ullr with a golden ring—his only piece of jewelry—along with the admonishment to always keep his word by it.

As the hour of banishment approached, only Odin's soft-spoken successor personally accompanied him to the Asgard frontier and bade him farewell, swearing his loyalty to the dethroned All-Father. In the years that followed, Ullr ruled with consistent wisdom and kindness, so much so that many of the Aesir spoke openly of making him their permanent lord and of imposing perpetual banishment on the absent Odin. Ullr, however, kept his own counsel in these matters, and no one could read his thoughts as he sometimes anxiously twisted the golden ring on his finger.

When, after nine years of wandering through the cosmos, the former Aesir king reappeared once more in Asgard, he was taken under

guard and brought to Valhalla's Hall of Judgment. "Where have you been all these many seasons," asked Ullr, still seated on the celestial throne, "and what have you seen or learned?"

Odin addressed the assembled gods and goddesses with dramatic accounts of his far-flung travels, the wonders he saw, and the wisdom he acquired.

When he had finished, Ullr rose from the seat he had occupied for the previous nine years. "You have used your time well, Odin, making you all the more worthy of retaking command. Even if this was not so, your rightful place is here. I swore it by my ring on the day you left us."

Now this short, simple speech so impressed the Aesir that even those who still harbored ill feelings against Odin were moved to wildly applaud and cheer his reinstatement, if only for the sake of noble Ullr. Tears glistened in All-Father's eye as he heartily shook hands with Ullr.

Reoccupying the throne, Odin spoke again as the king of Asgard: "My first proclamation is to accord Ullr full godhood, as signified by the power of this sacred stone." And he handed him a beautiful topaz. The immortals roared their approval until the very timbers of Valhalla shook with such gleeful noise.

To no one's surprise and his parents' immense pride, Ullr used his topaz well. With it, he created the northern lights, mindful of his own name—the Glorious One—bestowed on him at his birth by Sif. The aurora borealis was not only glorious to behold but also aided nighttime hunters like himself in shooting their prey. With his newly won divinity, he became the finest archer and built a humble palace, Ydalir, or Yew Dales, after the surrounding forest of yew, the trees of which he formed into the best long bows ever made.

Ullr usually went about on magical skis that permitted him cosmos-wide travel, thanks to the wisdom he learned firsthand from Odin. In the twelfth century *Gesta Danorum* (*The Danish History*, Book 3), by Saxo Grammaticus, a Christian historian, Ullr is described as "such a cunning wizard that he used a certain bone, which he had marked with awful spells, wherewith to cross the seas, instead of a vessel; and that by this bone he passed over the waters that barred his way as quickly as rowing."[1]

In time, he was revered as the god of winter itself, the divine patron of archery, hunting, and even skiing. As testimony to his general popularity and worship, many place-names derived from his name spread throughout Scandinavia, where Ullr's ship was for many centuries a poetic metaphor for "shield." In Norway the municipality of Akershus County is still known as Ullensaker, and Ullern and Ulleval are boroughs in Oslo. Ulleraker and Ullvi are today found in Sweden, where the image of Ullr, armed with a long bow while skiing, may still be seen on the eleventh-century Böksta Runestone.

Germany's Thorsberg Chape (a chape is the metal piece of a scabbard) is older by four hundred years and covered with an Elder Futhark inscription reading "priest of Ullr." Archaeological excavations during 2007 at Lilla Ullevi, the Little Shrine of Ullr, north of Stockholm, brought to light a fifteen-hundred-year-old shrine to the god. Unique throughout Scandinavia for the excellent state of its preservation, the structure contained sixty-five rings, symbols of Ullr, whose bond was his word.

Ullr's color is silver; his sacred stone is topaz. The classic, early-twentieth-century authority on the mystical lore of gemstones, George Frederick Kunz, repeats an ancient tradition: topaz was used as a talisman against nightmares and evil spirits of the underworld because of its association with the life-giving rays of the sun.[2] According to Guido von List, Ullr's rune signifies "resurrection, life after death," just as spring follows winter.[3] It incorporates, he says, the perennial advice, "Know yourself, then you will know all!" Rune master McVan believes it "teaches patience, endurance, courage."[4]

The glyph is beneficial whenever risk is involved. It stands for rapid, often unexpected changes—things the skier must know; the clearing away of one form to make way for another; the power to remove barriers. Ullr's rune heralds recuperation, stamina, and good health through the natural powers of resistance. It assures us that recovery from present physical ailments is inevitable. It is powered by strong emotions. Accordingly, as rune writer Lisa Peschel points out, his sign represents "the True Will of the querent—that thing he truly desires."[5] His rune implies that mortals who find it in their readings can expect promotion and an improved status in their work, together with additional responsibilities. It stands for duty fulfilled not under duress but through loyalty and a sense of right. All this is epitomized in Ullr's gracious fidelity to Odin and the happy consequences of his trust.

Its inverted image means that a chance to seize such an opportunity has been, or shortly will be, missed. The necessary vitality and willpower to achieve something better is lacking, perhaps because of a lingering illness. In male rune readers, sexual dysfunction from psychological or physiological causes is suggested. Even when reversed, however, Ullr's sign indicates dramatic changes, although of a less positive or pleasurable nature.

Ullr's time is Landvidi, generally synonymous in the modern zodiac with Capricorn, from December 21 to January 19, and Midwinter Day, the traditional midpoint of winter.

5

Thor

The Protector

Today the most famous—a thousand years ago the most popular—of the Norse gods, Thor is still renowned as the Thunderer. The lightning flashes we see above are the pathways of his hammer thrown in anger at his eternal enemies, the giants, hiding in ambush among black storm clouds (see color plate 2). He is the most powerful protector of Asgard and the bringer of luck, functions demonstrated when Mardal-Freya, the goddess of love and beauty, was alone gathering flowers in Midgard. She was about to return to her golden cart drawn by two white cats, when the dwarf Alberich surprised her. She naturally recoiled in disgust from the ugly, misshapen creature still grimy from his toils in the underworld. He smiled at her and was the very picture of conspiracy, but he held out before him the most magnificent necklace in the world. This was the renowned Brisingamen, the Ornament of the Brising. It was a splendid masterpiece comprising several bands of fine gold sparkling in broad rows of small, perfectly cut diamonds.

"Have no fear," Alberich said in his smoothest style. "Here, see if this fits. If so, you may want to buy it. For you, being who and what you are," he cooed obsequiously, "I'll sell it cheap."

Mardal-Freya was thrilled and almost reached for the necklace when suspicion alerted her. Something was wrong: "How did you get this?" she demanded. "It belongs to the Brising tribe's first woman, the wife of their chieftain."

"Ah, that is correct," Alberich explained with mock sympathy, "but she has since sadly passed away, and her man gave it to me as partial payment for a debt he owed. I don't really know why I accepted it. How could someone like me use such a beautiful thing?" and he laughed without mirth. Mardal-Freya should have guessed he was not telling the truth. His people were infamous as the Great Masters of the Lie. In fact, the necklace was cursed. Soon after Alberich sold it to the Brising, they found themselves in terrible debt, and their queen died mysteriously, strangling on something unseen. The jewelry was repossessed. But Mardal-Freya's instincts were blinded by the sight of the wonderfully worked gold and diamonds. She was thrilled to see them on her breast as Alberich lifted the fair mane of her hair and locked the Brisingamen with a tiny clasp behind her neck.

"There," he squawked in demented triumph. "You like it?"

"Yes, very much, indeed. What will you take for it?"

"That which I already possess: You! Follow me!" And he abused her with a litany of vile names, but Mardal-Freya was powerless now to respond or flee. She struggled furiously with the Brisingamen while Alberich laughed at her desperation. "You're wasting your time," her dark captor said. "It's permanently locked. I cannot open it, even if I wished. From now on, you have no choice but to do whatsoever I desire. Oh, we are going to have fun! And you will soon come to appreciate my better qualities," he sneered lasciviously.

He marched her all that day through fields and forests, until they came to a tall pile of immense boulders. These magically transformed themselves into the rough configuration of a living creature, a giant of stone. "Cute, isn't he?" Alberich taunted Mardal-Freya, but she looked away without speaking. "Hrungnir!" he called, and the ungainly colossus stood up to its full height, bearing a shield of stone. "See that we are not disturbed."

"What about my gold?" the monster asked in a voice like rocks crashing together in an avalanche.

"I'll bring it with me when I return with my fellow tribesmen.

There'll be a bonus for every intruder you kill. Understand?" The giant awkwardly hefted his ponderous shield as a mute response. The dwarf and the humiliated goddess passed between Hrungnir's legs to the edge of the Baltic Sea.

"Sit there," he almost yelled, as though commanding a dog, and she sank in despairing obedience on the sand. "I'm going to fetch my brothers. There's one for every diamond that twinkles in your Brisingamen. All of us will take our pleasure of you. When we're finished, whatever might be left of your mind or body will be thrown over the walls of Asgard. You and your high and mighty gods and goddesses! We Niflheimers were never good enough for you, were we? We'll show you all this time! If you won't allow us to rise to your heights, then we'll pull you down beneath our level. Then the world will see who rules it! Be patient, Mardal-Freya! Your lovers will be here soon! You might even get to like us, if you survive." Laughing, he ran off to tell his fellow dwarves the good news, admonishing Hrungnir once more to keep close guard.

Meanwhile, Mardal-Freya's empty golden cart had arrived at the foot of the rainbow bridge that leads to Asgard. Her two pure white cats that pulled the wagon meowed so piteously that Heimdall, the gate keeper, sounded his golden horn in alarm. A search for the missing goddess of love and beauty was immediately undertaken by all the Aesir and Asynir, aided by the Vanir and spirits of fallen heroes, even mortal men and women. But no one could find her.

Thor was among them. He quickly buckled Megin-gioerd, a broad belt that doubled his already prodigious strength, then he pulled on his powerful glove, Iarn Greiper (Iron Gripper). Snatching up his war hammer, Mjollnir, he leaped into a great, brazen chariot drawn by a pair of supernaturally huge he-goats. At the sound of his thunderous "Hiyah!" Tanngniortr and Tanngrrisnr bolted through the flung-open gates of Asgard and shot into the sky like Thor's own lightning bolts. His abundant mane of thick, red hair and his flaming red beard streamed in the wind from his angry face, as the enormous muscles of his massive arms and legs flexed in anticipation of combat with the giants, who surely abducted Mardal-Freya. He had no doubt they were responsible and itched to cleave their thick skulls for this high crime against heaven.

Below the whirling wheels of his chariot stretched the golden Baltic shore. "Might as well begin there," he decided, and dived down to come to a halt somewhat inland. Striding toward a rocky ridge, he was surprised to see it swiftly assemble itself into the image of an immense warrior. It towered before him menacingly, barring his passage. "Hrungnir," Thor laughed in recognition, "what are you made up for? I thought you were minding the sheep back in Jotenheim."

"Do not mock me," the giant growled like a monstrous child. "I warn you: Return home! You shall go no farther!"

"Who says so?" the jovial Aesir asked lightheartedly.

"All right, then. As you wish," Hrungnir bellowed. "Stay here forever!" And he threw his ponderous stone shield at the god. Thor jumped aside, as the rudely sculpted boulder crashed to the ground like an earthquake. Thor swung Mjollnir, letting it fly at the giant. The war hammer instantly ricocheted off Hrungnir's head after shattering it, and the moaning colossus tumbled to the ground in a rock slide of dead rubble.

Thor extended his iron-gloved right hand, yet Mjollnir did not return, as it always had in the past. He went looking for it, but he did not have far to search. Striker had lodged itself in the cleft of an outcrop near the seashore. As he worked his hammer from the rocks, he saw Mardal-Freya weeping on the beach, and he ran over to her. "Oh, brother," she cried, "I am lost, and it is because of my own greed." It was the Brisingamen, she confessed, that kept her enthralled to the detestable Alberich.

"The dwarf's curse is powerful," admitted Thor, "but not as strong as he would have everyone believe." With that, he made the sign of the four cardinal directions over Mardal-Freya with his war hammer, and the necklace fell from her to the ground. He picked it up with Iarn

Greiper, then flung the troublesome jewelry heavenward. It caught in the night sky, where it was known thereafter through Viking times as Brisingamen, today's Milky Way.

"But what are these?" Thor wondered, as he stooped to pick up light nodules of a kind of gold never seen before.

"While weeping here in my captivity," Mardal-Freya explained, "my teardrops fell into the salty sea, where they changed into ocean gold. As we go, I will transfer my sorrow into these trees along the shore. They will cry my sadness and shame into the water, making amber of the tree sap they shed. There is healing in these nuggets for anyone who seeks them."

As Thor escorted her to his celestial wagon, she let out a scream. A veritable army of hideous dwarves, her intended ravishers, were descending in their direction. They paused in amazement, however, before the huge corpse of their hired giant. While they still puzzled over the broken remains of Hrungnir, Thor leaped upon them in a rage, Mjollnir swinging in his hand. He crushed them like a boy squashing maggots with a toy hammer, although Alberich, the most cunning and cowardly of the lot, was first to escape the scene. "Stop!" Mardal-Freya exclaimed to Thor. "Do you want to exterminate the whole Niflheim race?"

"Gladly! But everyone is awaiting your return." After one more dwarf was smashed under Striker, almost as an afterthought, he whisked the goddess aboard, and the goat-drawn cart flew rapidly across the sky, following the rainbow bridge to Asgard. There, Mardal-Freya was the center of a heavenly homecoming. All the gods and goddesses, as well as the host of fallen heroes, celebrated her return, and praised her rescuer. "I was lucky that my hammer bounced off Hrungnir's head," he laughed, "and got lost among the rocks. Looking for it, I found Mardal-Freya."

"Luck always be with you," Odin toasted him with a full horn of mead, "and it will ever be with us!" The others echoed All-Father's toast, as Thor, grinning broadly, raised Mjollnir on high.

The profound antiquity and widespread esteem of Thor extended far beyond Scandinavia. He was worshipped in at least six major sanctuaries throughout England; Thurstable in Essex is an Anglicization of Thor's Pillar. According to Plutarch, the first-century-AD Greek historian, the Phoenician thunder deity was Thur, the bull, the same name by which the Normans, thousands of years later, revered the god.[1] The Germanic Thor was also described in the sagas as having "bellowed like a bull" whenever he swung his all-conquering hammer. Even in sixteenth-century Prussia, he was worshipped amid sacred groves that were off-limits to Christians. Some of his popularity may have stemmed from patronage by common people—yeomen and peasants—as opposed to Odin's association with the nobility.

Like his hair, Thor's color is red. His gem, the bloodstone, guards against deception, one of his reversed rune's negative characteristics. The bloodstone is traditionally and appropriately associated with thunder and lightning. Throughout Scandinavia, the rowan tree is sacred to him under the title of Thor's Deliverance. In Germany, he was said to have favored the oak with his thunderbolts. Late-twentieth-century scientists confirmed that oaks do indeed attract lightning, because they raise more quantities of water to a generally greater height than other trees. With Ullr and Odin, Thor shares Breidablikk, the astrological Broad Gleaming of Leo, from July 29 to August 13. This is a period of the most frequent annual thunderstorm activity in the Western world.

Thor's rune is the stylistic representation of Mjollnir, his short-handled Striker, the invincible war hammer only he can wield. Its image was reproduced in pre-Christian times and worn as a protective amulet around the neck, or in sacred ceremonies where meals or newborn infants were blessed with the sign of Thor. The gesture was eventually replaced by the similar sign of the Christian cross.

Like Thor himself, his rune stands primarily for protection, strength, vitality, and good luck. Its reverse signifies weakness, diminishing resistance, attenuated powers (physically, intellectually, emotionally, or spiritually), defenselessness, misfortune, or dwindling chances for success. We fail, for whatever reasons, to follow helpful advice or necessary guidance and overconfidently go our own way, oblivious to the pitfalls awaiting us. Justifiably or not, we may feel paranoid—that someone in an inferior or subordinate position is plotting against us. The reverse Thor rune warns of a challenge, difficult test, or danger. As McVan points out, "it employs the destructive force that is sometimes necessary in battling enemies and chaos, although it can also cause chaos."[2]

6

Aegir
The Oceanic God

Hjort captained a *knorr* sailing vessel carrying a full cargo of goods for the West Viking settlement in Iceland. To make the long voyage from Greenland as worthwhile as possible, he loaded on so many extra burdens of farm implements, tools, timber, furniture, and other commodities that his vessel rode too low in the water. Nevertheless, the midsummer season was usually mild, and he anticipated an uneventful crossing, as he and his crew had made many times before. In his avaricious haste to get under way, though, he neglected to offer so much as a word of prayer to the gods who watch over the affairs of men. Yet his unmindful oversight seemed to make no difference, as far as the voyage was concerned. Hjort cast off without incident to the waves and well-wishes of his family and those of the crew. The vessel was propelled by a favorable wind under a cloudless sky; the ship wallowed heavily but evenly with her well-secured, if overheavy, freight. Response at the tiller was sure but slow and sluggish. The weather held, however, as the stars brightly confirmed that Hjort was on course.

About midway to Iceland, however, the captain was alarmed to see a powerful storm rapidly approaching from the west, dead ahead. He steered directly for its center, folded his sail, and covered the decks. Rumbling ominously, the black clouds were flecked with purple lightning. In moments, the storm—the most violent that Hjort had ever experienced—was upon them. Over the din of rain and thunder, the helmsman yelled that he was losing control of the ship. She was taking on water from breakers crashing over her too-low freeboard. Captain and crew worked like mad men to unfetter the cargo. They unhesitatingly upended tables, chairs, bedsteads, and cabinets into the angry waters. Hammers, casks of nails, whole plows, harnesses, and enough timber to build a small town went over the side. Soon, there was nothing left, so they furiously worked their wooden pails, bailing the hull that was awash in rising seawater.

Gusts increased, infuriating the waves and causing them to batter the ship from side to side. Hjort joined the helmsman at the tiller—it needed the strength of both men to steer against the storm, which was gradually winning over their efforts to control the vessel. In the midst of this conflict between men and the elements, Hjort's voice rang out amid the peals of thunder and howling winds: "Aegir, who has brought this tempest to punish my greed and lack of piety, end your wrath; see us through to a safe landing somewhere, anywhere, and I will raise a monument to your clemency!" The sea god did not seem to hear his appeal. The gale raged throughout the night, and all hands labored to the utmost of their energies to save themselves from disaster. At times, the lolling knorr appeared on the verge of disintegrating or capsizing, because she was only sometimes under control.

With dawn, however, the storm blustered away into the east. The ship was still afloat, if barely, but its crew was too exhausted for celebration. Badly damaged, the vessel drifted for several weeks while Hjort and his men endeavored to make repairs and tried to determine their position. Still unsure where fate had blown them, they sighted land to the west and made for the coast. On shore, they found a thickly forested environment with freshwater streams. Fish and wild game were in abundance, and the climate was mild. Most surprising of all, lush grapevines grew everywhere—and so Hjort called the place Vinland.

Nor did he forget his promise to the sea god made at the height of the storm. After building temporary shelter and preserving food from the hunt, he joined his men in raising a three-story building near the coast where they landed. It was a round tower made of stone masonry and stood on eight arches with four small, square windows on the second story facing out on the cardinal directions. The structure was an observatory to sight the approach of ships and signal them with watch fires that warned of dangerous coastal rocks and shoals. But the loftier purpose—a monument to Aegir—was at once responsible for its creation and survival into modern times, for even today, so many centuries later, tourists and archaeologists from far and wide still visit and wonder about the forgotten origins of Rhode Island's Newport Tower.

Aegir's name derives from the Old Gothic word for "water": *ahwa*. He is the god of the Midgard ocean, at the bottom of which sprawls his enormous palace. Its vast halls are ornate with the spoils of sunken ships amid profuse decorations of coral, shell, and pearl.

As the sea over which he reigns represents the subconscious mind, so the Aegir rune signifies unconscious emotions and instinctual action or reaction. It is also powerfully protective, the harbinger of new and fortunate influences that are often related to solid friendships or enduring partnerships—not unlike Aegir's storm that brought the Norsemen to their higher destiny on the pre-Columbian shores of the North American continent. Part of the sea god's protection is in the form of strong premonitions or subtle warnings, formerly known as omens and today regarded as meaningful coincidences. His rune image resembles someone with open arms or a person in a pose of worship (see color plate 4). It is better known as Neptune's trident, the emblem of numerous marine deities—all Indo-European cultural inflections of the same sea god. Appropriately, rune investigator Nigel Pennick associates the color of Aegir's rune with dark blue, like that of the azure sea.[1]

Its triune symbol stands for spiritual synthesis, the reconciliation of matter and spirit with godhood—a meaning also found in the sacred trident of the Greek sea god, Poseidon, ruler of the unconscious; the three-pronged scepter of Siva, the Hindu Master of Creation, signifying his omniscient Third Eye; and the three-pronged weapon of the Roman *retiarius* (gladiator), who, with his net, was the sacred impersonator of Neptune. The sea-god's characteristic fishing net and trident were duplicated in the same objects used by gladiators.

Aegir's trident rune generally corresponds in the modern zodiac to Capricorn—appropriately enough, the astrological "Seagoat"—beginning December 28 and ending January 19, Midwinter Day, the traditional midpoint of winter. To the Norse, this period was associated with Landvidi, the White Land, a clear reference to Atlantis, the lost civilization that sank beneath the sea during a natural catastrophe at the close of the Bronze Age, thirty-two hundred years ago. The Hindu Mahabharata and Vishnu Purana both describe the sunken White Island as Atala, called Atland in Northern Europe, as cited in the Frisian *Oere Linda Bok*.[2] Literally, The Book of What Happened in the Old Time, it is a compilation of ancient Frisian oral histories transcribed for the first time around AD 1256 and finally published in Holland during 1871. Aegir's underwater palace is an apparent mythic correlation to the drowned capital, where the runes and their divination magic were believed to have originated.

Thanks to Thor, who stole it from the giants, Aegir owns the largest cauldron in the world. A mile across, it is the ancient vessel of infinite abundance. It was Christianized and radically downsized during medieval times as the Holy Grail. Like this cauldron, Aegir's rune signifies the boundless possibilities of fresh influences and suggests a connection between gods and men. Upright, it embodies life itself, stylistically resembling a human with arms upraised. In fact, it is commonly known as the Life Rune. Its inversion, with arms slumped toward the earth, signifies death, the dissolution of forms, extinction, or the necessary end no one—not even the gods—can avoid. This concept is exemplified in Aegir's rune stone, the black tourmaline, symbolizing the dark depths of the ocean and psyche that are his realm. His queen is Ran, who, regarding life and death, shares some influential features with his rune.

Like the sea that Aegir personifies, his sign alternates between life and death. More usually, an inverted Aegir rune implies that something must end, enabling a fresh start. It can also suggest deception—even bad guidance or betrayal—practiced by those around us. Seemingly attractive opportunities may be in reality snares to defraud or mislead us. Vulnerability pervades this inverted glyph. The negative side of Aegir's rune cautions vigilance and discretion. At such times we must learn to trust our instinct but also be on guard against potential dangers.

7

Ran

Goddess of the Sea

Although the Norse claimed descent from Askr and Embla, the first man and woman transformed by All-Father Odin from a pair of trees, their earliest home as a people was on Atland, after which the Atlantic Ocean was named. The island was known for its great mountain, At, the Upholder of the Heavens, appearing thus when overcast skies obscured the summit. Atland was rich in forest timber with which to build the first ships. The soil was so fertile that two crops could be harvested each year, and the air was always mild and temperate. For many years, the Norse forefathers lived in peace and plenty.

But one day the mountain of At, tired of supporting its celestial burden for so long, exploded under geologic pressures and collapsed into the sea, dragging Atland, along with most of its inhabitants, into oblivion. The few survivors of the catastrophe took to their ships, narrowly escaping with their lives and little else. Once out upon the now-vacant ocean, they prayed to Ran—the goddess of the sea, Aegir's queen—for mercy and guidance (see color plate 3). She took pity on them, and appeared in the dreams of their leaders, the brothers Nefthuns and Inka. "Go toward the direction you feel is right," she told them, "and you will find a happy destiny." After they awoke from sleep, the brothers were surprised to learn that they shared the same dream, but they could not agree on the right direction. Nefthuns wanted to sail eastward, toward the European continent, which seemed the only sensible thing to do, but Inka thought they should follow the sun westward across uncharted seas, "to honor the goddess with our bravery, rather than seek safety with less boldness."

Unable to agree between themselves, the brothers gave the decision to the surviving Atlanders. Somewhat more than half sided with Nefthuns, and they soon reached that narrow passage where the tips of Africa and Europe almost meet. Sailing into the Mediterranean, they reestablished their worship of Fasta, the Earth Mother, which later generations of Romans venerated at the Temple of Vesta. Nefthuns and his followers voyaged farther eastward, and a princess named Min-erva from the old religion of Atland founded Athens. After her death, she was worshipped as the Greek goddess Minerva. Nefthuns steered along the shores of North Africa, settling at what became Tunisia, named in his honor. Following his death, the Etruscans named their sea god after him: Nefthuns later became the Roman Neptune.

His brother, with a smaller contingent, sailed to the west and was never heard of again. But his name—Inka—suggests he, like Nefthuns, was a culture founder who bequeathed his name to subsequent generations, this time in South America, where they became the Incas of Peru and Bolivia. In both cases, Ran had blessed the survivors of drowned Atland with fortuitous voyages that ended in long-lasting prosperity.

Just so, her rune signifies positive movement or travel. It speaks of a journey we will soon undertake. As Svensson points out, however, such travels are not be limited to physical relocation from place to place, but instead may imply an inner journey of illumination.[1] Caution should be thrown to the winds. Be brave, have some guts, and "follow your bliss," as Joseph Campbell exhorted his students.[2] The time has come to move on and *get* on with your life. Ran's upright sign is a portent for change. In fact, the word *revolution* begins with the first letter of the goddess's name, and, as McVan insists, stands for right action and order.[3]

According to Kunz, Ran's gemstone is the jacinth: "especially recommended as an amulet for travelers."[4] Its reputation to grant those who wear it a cordial reception as a welcome guest echoes Ran's hospitality for those who die at sea. This transparent jewel of the zircon family is also associated with the prudent conduct of business affairs. In addition, jacinth is Ran's glyph because both are red in color. Her rune belongs to Sokkvabekk, August 29 to September 30, within the zodiacal sign of Virgo.

Paralleling the story of Nefthuns and Inka, Svensson asserts that Ran signals a "time to leave behind the 'I'm in two minds' scenario and make a decision."[5] Her energies are propitious for reasonable discussions or amicable negotiations from which everyone may benefit, in much the same way Nefthuns and Inka settled their disagreement about the proper interpretation of a common dream. In terms of business, the appearance of Ran's symbol declares that the optimum moment to buy or sell has arrived or is soon coming. Critical information or an important message is either on its way or has just been received.

Ran owns a magic net of far-flung powers. In it, she can gather the natural abundance of the sea (*net*working), or, should her rune be reversed, drown those who risk their fortunes on the wave-tossed surface of her vast realm. An old Viking belief held that if the ghosts of drowning victims appeared at their own funerals, they have been given a good welcome and handsome banquet by Ran in her underwater palace among the sunken ruins of Atland. Failure to take proper countermeasures to her upside-down rune, however, could lead to misunderstanding, disagreements, arguments, ensnaring contracts better left unsigned, "hell rides," unpleasant voyages or journeys, and shipwreck in every sense of the word. Like the sea personified by the goddess, she is capable of either carrying us toward good fortune and happiness or drowning our chances for success. Fishermen may earn a good living from the catches they make, but sailors who ignore the signs of bad weather ahead do so at their peril.

8

Kvasir

The Divine Inspirer

There was a time when the Aesir numbered only five gods. During this early period, they fell into fighting with their brother immortals, the Vanir, over the proper development of the world that both groups had just brought into being. Realizing that their conflict would eventually lead to the destruction of all Creation, they solemnly swore never to go to war against each other again and vowed henceforth to settle amicably all differences among themselves. To solemnize their peace, each god spat once into a ceremonial vase. They had no sooner done so, though, when a new deity sprang fully matured into their presence. His name, he said, was Kvasir, the spirit of wise generosity. He was kind and gentle, filled with wonderful knowledge and goodness (see color plate 6). Both Aesir and Vanir came to honor deeply and respect his counsel, which he gave freely to immortals and death-doomed humans alike.

Although an honored place among the Vanir was set aside for him, Kvasir often roamed Midgard, the realm of men and women—always, like Odin, disguised as a congenial traveler and sharing what he knew. If he found welcome at even the humblest home, he enjoyed relaxing by the hearth fire, where he amply rewarded his hosts with friendly wisdom. Thus, through his widespread generosity, humankind arose gradually from savagery to civility.

Kvasir was of inestimable value to the Aesir, as well. One of their own had committed a barbarous act that demanded punishment. But

Loki, the culprit, was a master of shapeshifting disguises that deceived even the gods. Playing the private detective, Kvasir followed subtle clues left by the elusive criminal to an abandoned hovel, where the remains of a recently extinguished fire still smoldered in the hearth. Sifting through the ashes, his fingers drew forth a badly burned web. He recognized it as the remains of a fisherman's net, part of a shamanistic ritual for physical transformation. Kvasir returned at once to Asgard, where he announced that Loki had assumed the identity of a salmon. Armed with this information, the fugitive was apprehended.

For his services, however, Kvasir did not receive due reward. To the Niflheim dwarves, the greater the soul, the deeper their hatred, so they murdered Kvasir by cutting his throat and drinking his blood. To sweeten their monstrous feast, they mixed Kvasir's blood with honey. The combination resulted in mead, a magical brew that inspired poetry in whoever tasted it. The dwarves corrupted its use, though, to mock their betters, which led them to trouble with the giants, who left the dwarves to drown on a low rock far out at sea. The squealing Niflheimers bribed their way out of this otherwise terminal situation by handing over the mead to their captors—but the oafish residents of Jotunheim further abused their newfound skill in singing bawdy songs and guffawing at ribald doggerel.

By rights, Kvasir's remains belonged to the Aesir, so Odin, disguised as an irresistibly handsome field hand, visited the giantess assigned to guard Kvasir's honeyed blood hidden deep inside a mountain. In exchange for three nights of lovemaking, she allowed him three drinks of the potent brew. These were enough for him to consume every drop. Shapeshifting himself into an eagle, Odin flew back to Asgard, where he regurgitated the mead. It was properly used thereafter to inspire true poetry and song that appealed, as all art should, to the higher nature and ideal sentiment of everyone who experiences it.

Exceptional poets, singers, and musicians were said to have been blessed by Odin with a drop or two of the celestial mead. The name of the Old German *kvas,* a strong beer, was derived from Kvasir, and the word is still current in Jutland, used to describe the juice of crushed fruits that go into the production of mead.

Like the brew that flowed from Kvasir's sacrifice, his rune is associated with the spark of inspiration that artists and craftsmen require to materialize the images locked in their hearts and minds. It is, in fact, synonymous with creativity, the birth of ideas and concepts, that fire in the imagination that transforms inner abstraction into physical reality. Here, Kvasir's glyph is suggested by the indistinct strands he found in the fireplace. In his hands they revealed something greater. Kvasir's generous spirit is the kernel of all real art, which strives to elevate every soul that comes into contact with it. Artists must achieve, during at least some moment in the creative process, an altered state of consciousness occasionally perceived by outsiders as a form of madness. Appropriately, Pennick observes that Kvasir's rune represents "the borderline between madness and genius," and associates it with illumination, knowledge, learning, insight, remembrance, and wisdom.[1]

Peschel writes that his symbol implies, as Kvasir himself did, "the friendly, warm, controlled flame of the torch or the hearth fire."[2] His is the torch of enlightenment through inspirational art. As such, it represents a fundamental creative energy not unrelated to vigorous good health and strong powers of recuperation. It signifies new, positive things and urges us to open ourselves to their consideration. Because he was so giving of his wisdom and goodness, his glyph often represents gift-giving and altruism. It also connotes regeneration through sacrifice.

The rune's "gemstone" is the mineral flint, from which we may strike sparks that kindle a blaze of light. Accordingly, Kvasir's color is fire red. His place in the astrological scheme of the cosmos is the Norse equivalent of Libra, known as Glitnir, the Hall of Splendor, from September 23 to October 22. Reversed, Kvasir's rune means loss, coldness, sadness, weakness, emptiness, declining health, miserliness, a paucity of ideas, and dwindling creativity.

9

Gefion

The Sacred Benefactor

There was once a North Teuton king, not really a bad man, whose prosperity had nonetheless blinded him to the impoverishment of his own subjects. At their expense, he acquired numerous tracts of land, which formed the basis for his vast wealth. The common people were forced to farm small pastures and fields that were barely sufficient to scratch out a living.

When the king and his court were casting the runes as an amusing after-dinner entertainment one evening, the runes all came up negative for the ruler, who at once recognized their purport. He was being warned against the perils of greed, but he brushed them aside as so much superstition. The next day, the prince and heir to the throne took deathly sick. Skilled physicians and even renowned sorcerers from distant lands were summoned to restore the boy's health, but no one was able to help him.

The king pleaded with the gods for mercy, and, as though in swift answer to his prayers, a ragged old woman who promised to cure his son appeared at the gate of the great hall. "My name is Gefion, majesty, and, if you will allow me the opportunity, I can save your son."

"Do that," he exclaimed, "and I will give you anything you want."

"You may decide my reward," she said, "according to your honest judgment."

Under her care, the lad's health was restored in a short time, and the whole kingdom rejoiced at his miraculous recovery. "You have done well," the king told her, but his avaricious mind was filled with cunning. Seeing that the grimalkin was hardly strong enough to walk unaided, he said, "You may have as much of my land as you can plow in a day." And his fawning courtiers laughed with him at the old nurse.

"To do with as I see fit?" Gefion asked him in a feeble voice.

"Absolutely," he chuckled.

She thanked him, then shuffled from the hall to the mockery of the king and his yes-men.

When she eventually reached his richest land, the doddering crone put her hand to a waiting plow. As soon as she touched the handle, she seemed possessed of superhuman strength. Faster than any team of the most powerful horses, she raced around the field as great plumes of soil arched high behind her incredible progress. Onlookers were amazed, and the king, hearing their exclamations of disbelief, hurried to see for himself. The old woman had already excavated a vast ring and connected it via a beautiful stone canal to the local river. The artificial torrent filled the ditch with water, creating an enormous moat and surrounding a sizable island. This done, she went on to claim additional territories with her plow. Its steel glowed like a sword blade in the furnace, so great was the speed with which Gefion literally flew across the realm, claiming one huge tract of land after another. By sundown, the entire kingdom, not excluding the palace, had been newly parceled out and belonged to her.

"You have dispossessed me," the king sobbed in belated recognition of the goddess he had offended. "I'm ruined!"

"Not so," she answered kindly. "You have brought all this upon yourself. Otherwise, my presence here would not have been necessary. I hold you to your promise, that I may dispose of my lands any way I see fit. All of them outside this circular ditch henceforth revert to your people. Remove your hall to that little island. That is your new citadel. Consider yourself fortunate, because I could reduce you to beggary, if I so choose. The love of your subjects will be far more rewarding than any other riches you owned."

The chastised king relocated to his humbler estate on the small island, from which he ruled in generosity and fairness, and his people responded as the goddess foretold. Moreover, now that they were allowed to possess their own land, their productivity was so great that the hitherto miserly monarch was himself borne along on a general wave of prosperity. Gefion had lived up to her name—the Giver—for all concerned.

Her rune, accordingly, signifies gifts or the act of giving. It is an entirely positive sign and cannot be reversed or made upside-down to indicate negativity of any kind. The glyph may also mean that apparent difficulties, even perceived calamities, are actually gifts in the temporary disguise of trouble or loss. Svensson does sensibly caution, however, that nothing in life is completely free and that with gifts come responsibilities.[1] Giving and generosity imply linked behavior, so Gefion might be telling us in her rune cast that, in order to receive gifts, we must ourselves be generous. McVan rightly comments that reciprocity, as the North Teuton king learned, "binds a leader to his followers. This was the idea behind sacrifices or gifts to the gods, which should bring favors in return."[2] We can hardly expect munificence from heaven if we are niggardly with the needs of our fellow human beings.

An old Anglo Saxon poem begins, "Giving is an ornament that displays worth."[3] Part of that personal worth includes the graciousness with which we accept a gift. Pennick affirms that Gefion "symbolizes unity between the donor and the person to whom the gift is given, creating a state of balance and harmony."[4] This concept is explicit in the rune itself: two strokes are united in a new image.

Astrologically, the rune parallels Libra, September 23 to October 22, in the Norse Hall of Splendor, or Glitner. Gefion's rune is azure; jade, her gemstone. These, as French symbolist J. E. Cirlot pointed out, represent "power, spirituality and sublimation."[5] Azure signifies dignity in giving and receiving. It is the color of jade, a stone once used as a grave good, a parting gift from the realm of the living to the beloved dead.

10

Vidar

Conqueror of Doom

Second only to their last combat at the end of the world, the first battle undertaken by the Aesir was their greatest. They had to overcome the frost giant, Ymir, if life was to survive and evolve. Their fight was led by Odin, but it was Vidar who dealt the fatal blow. It unleashed the Great Flood that purged static eternity to usher in a new age of nature and civilization. Yet by setting in motion the process of time, all things come into being and inevitably are crushed from existence in the same mechanism. Vidar foresaw a Twilight of the Gods, an inevitable end to the magnificent epoch they created to last for a thousand-thousand years.

Vidar determined to survive that imminent cataclysm and help rebuild the world in a distant future that he could not envision but intuitively knew existed in the irreversible cycles of death and rebirth. From the Norns, Vidar learned the part he was ordained to play in that last battle between the forces of light and darkness. The Norns were three female spirits who wove among themselves the web of fate that not even a god may break. They told him that Fenris, the cosmic wolf—the most terrifying phenomenon in the universe—would some day menace the Aesir as the ultimate threat to their existence. This was the terrible monster-of-monsters that Vidar had been assigned by destiny to fight. If not stopped in time, Fenris would devour all hope for a renewal of life after Ragnarok.

For that far-off combat Vidar devised a defense against his apparently invincible opponent. He shared neither his developing strategy nor the Norns' secret predictions of doom for fear the dwarves and their army of benighted giants would use the information to their advantage on the Last Day. Henceforward, Vidar was known as the Silent God (see color plate 8). His silence was no less perplexing to friends and enemies alike than his unusual, personal collection: Disguised as an indigent priest, he often went among the shoemakers of Midgard, begging them for snips of leather they ordinarily discarded after shaping the heel and toe for all kinds of footwear, from boots to buskins. It would be good of them to donate these unwanted pieces, he piously explained, for Asgard's war effort against the gargantuan Jotunheimers and conniving Niflheimers.

Shoemakers heartily gave the shapeshifting Vidar all the otherwise useless remainders he could carry, until he possessed enough leather to fashion the most impenetrable pair of military boots ever devised. They went high up his legs, covering most of his thighs, and their soles were of an unprecedented thickness. He tried them on; they fit perfectly. To these he added a pair of heavy leather gauntlets, which protected not only his hands but went so far as to reach almost his elbows. Boots and gloves he then set aside until they would be needed during the ultimate confrontation.

The day of its onset came at last, as the badly outnumbered gods fought against overwhelming hordes that stormed from the depths of Hela's infernal realm. These stampeded across the luminous rainbow bridge toward the very gates of Asgard. At every step they were opposed by the Aesir and Vanir, with their own elite troops of heroes. The enemy mobs were decimated, but wave after wave of attackers pressed on behind the growing mounds of dead giants and dwarves, until even the defenders of heaven began to fall or retreat. Infuriated by the catastrophic struggle he was missing, Fenris, howling, broke from his chains and descended like a blazing comet on Asgard. He broke down its gates and attacked All-Father himself. Odin fought valiantly against the monstrous wolf, which nonetheless succeeded in devouring the god.

Distracted by the life-and-death combat in which he was so violently engaged, Vidar missed his chance to save the king of heaven. Rage and shame nearly burst his heart, as he marched up to the huge enemy of the world. Its mouth gaped wide like a cave of oversized fangs and lolling tongue, ready to swallow another deity whole. Vidar unhesitatingly jumped inside, planting his leather-shod feet firmly in the astonished creature's lower jaw. Then, with his gloved hands, he pushed with something greater than all his strength against the roof of Fenris's mouth, breaking the salivating jaws and tearing them apart in a cracking explosion of blood and agony. With a gurgling shriek heard throughout the cosmos, Fenris collapsed. His dying carcass fell into the sea, compelling the waters to rise in waves that drowned Midgard and overflowed Asgard, extinguishing the flames of battle and washing the illimitable dead away into unknown graves.

Yet there were some survivors—a few human beings and fewer gods who found refuge on the summits of high mountains. Among this handful of the living was Vidar. Together, they began the task of building a new world.

Despite the apparent mayhem of his myth, Vidar's rune is generally associated with joy. Svensson writes that Vidar with epitomizes the old adage, "All's well that ends well."[1] More specifically, however, his is the inner joy or soul's calm and tranquillity when we communicate with our own godhood, as Vidar did when he foresaw his destiny in the Ragnarok. The Silent God refers to his wisdom or vision through meditation. As Guido von List observed,

> [T]o be with one's Self is to be with God. As long as a people possesses unspoiled their entire original ability to internalize as a natural [i.e., not overcivilized] people, it also has no cause to worship an external divinity. For an external divine service bound by ceremony is only made obvious when one is not able to find God in one's own

innermost being, and begins to see this outside his ego and outside
the world—"in there, in the starry heaven." The less internal the
person is, the more outward his life becomes. The more a people
loses its sense of inner worth, the more pompous and ceremonialized
its outward manifestations become. . . .[2]

The Norse, a "natural" people secure in their instinctual relationship with the gods, had no need for dogma, a hierarchical church structure, or cathedral buildings. They were interested in spirituality, not
religion; a mystical experience that put them in accord with Creation,
not a man-made doctrine aimed at making them tithe-paying congrega-
tionalists. As such, all they needed for spiritual fulfillment were their
myths and the rituals to reenact them at sacred sites outdoors. Vidar
personifies this nonstructured outlook, because his worship was among
the least formalized yet most beloved of the gods. Common people paid
him homage during the course of their daily lives, rather than in oper-
atic church services. As late as the thirteenth century Swedish shoemakers regularly put aside scraps of leather on behalf of the god, wishing
him good luck in his upcoming confrontation with Fenris.

Astrologically, the Silent God occupies a position within Libra, from
September 23 to October 22, known in Norse as the Hall of Splendor,
Glitnir. Vidar's color is yellowish gold, like his gemstone: chrysolite.
Defense against nightmarish opposition, such as Vidar encountered in
Fenris, is attributable to both his jewel and its color.

Vidar's rune is the emblem of meditation, that quiet state through
which we enter into the pure joy of our innermost being. As he over-
came the monster, so too his glyph means success for the person who
draws it. McVan observes that his sign "battles against discouragement
and sadness to bring cheerfulness and courage in both the individual
and the group. Clan-centric and binding of kin, this is the rune of emotional healing and self-confidence, the will to win."[3] All these characteristics are, of course, exemplified in Vidar's myth. So too, his survival of
the Ragnarok deluge on the summit of a mountain is paralleled in the

significance of his glyph, which "signifies both a conclusion and a new beginning: the mountain-top has been reached, and so there is much happiness, but at the same time new vistas open up and new challenges wait to be conquered."[4]

A reversed Vidar rune urges a solid attempt at meditation in order to clear the mind and go within for the direction we lack. We are unhappy because our plans—from which we could be expecting too much—are not working out as we hoped. The best move may be to postpone any important decision until a more favorable moment arrives. In any case, caution is advised.

11

Heimdall
He of the Echoing Horn

The sea god Aegir and Ran, his queen, had an only child, a son, they called Heimdall. For nursemaids, they entrusted him to "nine giant maids on the edge of the Earth," as the skalder sang in the ancient *Voluspa Saga*.[1] Because these giantesses were identified with various kinds of waves that rolled across Aegir's vast domain, they transformed the lad's hair to wavy white, as a token of their care that he would possess for as long as he lived.

More importantly, they imbued him with sensitivities unknown to any other creature. The eagle himself could perceive only a fraction of the distances Heimdall was able to see clearly, even at night. This was fortuitous, because he needed less sleep than a bird. His hearing was so acute that he could detect the sound of grass or sheeps' wool growing on the other side of the world. His foster mothers may have lent him something of their size, too, because Heimdall grew up to have not only Ran's fair features and the dignity of King Aegir, but also he was most powerfully built and of greater stature than Odin, hitherto the tallest of the Aesir.

Learning of these extraordinary gifts, All-Father asked him to fill a very important position. "Bifrost is a rainbow bridge that connects Midgard to Asgard," he explained. "It is the means by which most of us travel back and forth from our palaces to the world of humankind. In former times, it was safe for any of us to use. But now we are threatened by the envious dwarves and giants. We are not frightened of them, but it is impossible, even for us, to always watch over our goddesses. Bifrost needs a guardian. Can we count on you?"

Heimdall naturally felt honored by this request from the king of the gods, but it was chiefly his sense of duty that urged him to accept at once. For parting gifts he received from his father, Aegir, an immense broadsword made with superb skill from the resmelted iron rivets of sunken ships that littered the ocean floor. Mother Ran gave her son the Gjallarhorn, a golden Echoing Horn magnificently embossed with animated representations of life in the sea. The nine giant maids, having already given him all they could, wished him farewell.

When the towering Heimdall was introduced to all the Aesir, Asynir, and Vanir, they good-naturedly welcomed him as the White God for his fair, wavy hair. To show they meant him no disrespect, they presented him with a suit of shining white armor, the only one of its kind. But it was as the Watcher that he took up his station at Bifrost's highest point, from which he could look out over all Creation. Here he built his sturdy castle, Himinbjorg, the Cliffs of Heaven. It was the world's most impregnable fortress and a home for the Vanir, who loved him as one of their own. Heimdall was henceforth the guardian of all the gods. No dwarf was cunning enough to get by him, and the giants, who recognized something of themselves in his great strength, felt intimidated, not least of all because of the massive iron sword at his side. Whenever a god or goddess began ascending the rainbow bridge to Asgard, Heimdall blew the Gjallarhorn to announce ceremoniously his or her arrival. Its golden tone echoed musically throughout all the halls of heaven.

One night, he heard something buzzing in the direction of Mardal-Freya's bedroom. The goddess was about to be robbed of her jewels by the trickster god, Loki, in the guise of a fly. The ever-alert Heimdall, however, snatched the insect in mid-flight and flung it out of Asgard.

Sometimes, Heimdall was approached by mortal men or women, even young lads, who begged his permission to pass. They wanted to leave the troubles of their world for Asgard, where they would promise to do anything that was asked of them. The Watcher invariably turned them away, but never without kindness and even sympathy. He occasionally took the time to tell them that their destiny, which was known to the gods, lay in Midgard and nowhere else. Everything would come to pass in time, he assured them. All they needed was patience. What seemed to them the delay of their hopes was actually part of the process of their fulfillment. "No one may run ahead of his or her fate," he liked to quote Odin, before gently sending them on their way back into the world of struggle and illusion. Heimdall loyally guarded his post over the course of many human generations. Neither Niflheimer nor Jotunheimer nor a single gate-crashing mortal ever set foot in heaven while he was in charge of the rainbow bridge—that is, until the coming of Ragnarok.

As soon as the massed forces of destruction began their invasion, Heimdall saw and heard them. He sounded his Gjallarhorn in alarm, thereby giving the gods precious time to assemble their defenses. When the foes at last attacked Bifrost, Heimdall stood up to them alone, hacking with his huge iron sword into the hate-crazed mobs. Fresh corpses, severed limbs, bones, blood, and screams flew in all directions from his ringing blade. Although he delighted in the slaughter of so many enemies, the dull weight of their inextinguishable numbers forced him back, step by step toward the gates of Himinbjorg. Through them now streamed all the gods and heroes to his aid. Their opponents fell in masses of dead and dying invaders, but for every one slain, ten more took his place.

The invaders pushed into Valhalla itself, setting all ablaze with a forest of torches. Heimdall battled with still greater fury among the bright flames consuming Odin's doomed hall when he saw Loki, the former Aesir responsible for this catastrophe. The White God strode in a few determined paces to the traitor. "Thus is All-Father avenged!" he cried. A vengeful swing of his iron sword split Loki in half from crown to crotch. At that same moment, Valhalla's great roof collapsed, crushing to death thousands of combatants, giants and gods alike.

Heimdall is associated with the Joyous Home of the gods, Gladsheim, from October 28 to November 13, within Scorpio. His color is blue for both the sea from which he came and his destiny in the sky, at the highest point of the rainbow bridge. Cirlot underscores this significance by pointing out that blue belongs to the rarefied atmosphere of the clear sky, implying far-seeing vision.[2] The White God's symbolism is further elaborated in Heimdall's gemstone, quartz crystal, used for scrying (prophecy and other forms of spiritual vision achieved by meditating on a crystal or a similarly translucent medium). He was, after all, known as the Watcher. His incompletely preserved myth recounts that he obtained a particularly precious quartz crystal as soon as he killed Loki, although precisely how it was won, its particular significance, or what became of it is unknown.

Heimdall's spiritual essence is wonderfully expressed in his rune. It counsels patience to delays put in our path for reasons we do not often understand. We must learn to trust that everything that happens to us—both positive and negative—is part of the process of life, the means and mechanism by which human growth can take place. Apparent disappointments that seem discouraging or even catastrophic when they occur in the narrow context of our day-to-day struggles are later seen from the perspective of hindsight as essential features in our personal development. Heimdall defines the precise limits of our particular situation.

Although his rune stands for limitations, these are the sometimes temporary, but always unavoidable, consequences of living in the physical world. The appearance of his glyph may warn of a setback or impediment to our plans. Heimdall counsels endurance, fortitude, forbearance, self-mastery, and trust in our own destiny. Guido von

List believed the sign of the White God offered opportunities for introspection when we are confronted with some immovable delay: "Introspective awareness and endurance produce a high self-confidence in the power of the personal spirit which dwells within all persons and a power which can persuade a strong spirit to believe in it without any doubt."

12

Njord
The Needful

There was once a small but charming fishing village in an isolated bay on the south coast of Norway. For many generations, most of its few residents made a modest, sufficient living from the sea. Although by no means wealthy, they were content, and delighted in the quiet beauty of their surroundings, glad to be unknown by the outside world. Eventually, however, they tired of their simple existence and longed for the wealth enjoyed elsewhere. They hit upon a scheme to improve their situation: they rumored it about that the bay fronting their village contained larger concentrations of fish than any other place in all Scandinavia. "Who knows," they sniggered among themselves, "it might even be true." Their objective was to attract fishermen from far and wide and charge a fixed fee, even renting boats and equipment at inflated prices.

Sure enough, outsiders began arriving at the little coastal town, happy to pay for the privilege of angling in its adjoining, supposedly abundant waters. Because the newcomers were generally satisfied with their catch, word spread of the new, rich fishing grounds to be plied. The trickle of visitors soon grew into swarms, and the villagers abandoned their former ways of making a living. No longer interested in the hard labor of fishermen or farmers, they became dealers in tackle, line, hooks, bait, and boats. Everyone was commercially involved and collecting more silver coins than each ever dreamed possible.

Meanwhile, the fields lay fallow, and only strangers launched their boats from the beach. The little village began to deteriorate, because no one bothered anymore about its local crafts or arts save those shoddy, hastily made items that could be quickly sold. No one seemed to care, because everyone was more interested in making money. By autumn, however, a change took place in their lucrative state of affairs. There were no more visitors for a single, obvious reason: too many anglers had overfished the bay. Its waters were now deserted. With winter in the offing, the villagers were suddenly faced with starvation. Even the few one-time farmers had abandoned the soil for new careers as tradesmen, so no stocks of food had been stored. Mortified, the villagers had no other choice but to buy fish caught in their own bay by the same outsiders who, understandably, now charged exorbitant prices for even the most undesirable specimens. The silver coins that had flowed so freely during the previous summer now went to purchase bare subsistence.

During the winter solstice festival, which celebrates the gradual return of the sun after the longest night of the year, the villagers cried out to their most beloved deity, Njord, to pity them in their need. He was the god of seamanship, the divine patron of sailors and maritime peoples who mediated between them and the often difficult sea god and sea goddess, Aegir and Ran. Njord heard the villagers' prayer, but he would not heed it.

"Let them relearn those skills that sustained them and their forefathers!" he raged in Noatun, his palace, the Enclosure of Ships, at the bottom of the ocean. "More important, let them remember who they once were. I will not be their teacher. The need they themselves created out of their own avarice will instruct them. Let them learn from it or perish, for all I care!"

And so the villagers agonized through the worst winter they ever knew, pressed by starvation and abandoned by their god. With difficulty, they survived the long months of snow and frost. By spring, all their money was gone—spent for basic survival. Yet, they learned their lesson, and immediately set about reviving the dilapidated town. Farmers returned to their neglected fields and livestock, while fishermen tentatively pushed off into the somewhat ice-free bay with meager hope that perhaps a fish or two might have strayed into its depleted waters.

Njord had followed the old, quiet dignity with which the people

had endured the winter, and he was favorably impressed by their determination to restore their former way of life. He caused more fish than
ever before to fill the bay's deep, cold, azure waters, and the villagers
rejoiced at his generosity, which they thereafter honored in a special,
annual spring festival. Moreover, from then on, whenever strangers passing through inquired, "How's the fishing around here?" they invariably
replied with the same, discouraging white lie: "Terrible!"

Peschel writes that Njord's rune "always indicates a time of passing through
a difficult learning situation. This time is known as 'crossing the abyss'.
. . ."[1] It could mean a health problem, but invariably some kind of necessity
is at issue. Indeed, McVan refers to it by its ancient title: "the need rune."[2]
Guido von List quotes an old German saying, "The need-rune blossoms
on the nail of the Norn"—one of the spinners of inexorable destiny.[3]

> This is not "need" (distress) in the modern sense of the word, but
> rather the "compulsion of fate" that the Norns fix according to primal
> laws. With this, the organic causality of all phenomena is to be under-
> stood . . . he commands knowledge of the future and also understands
> how to settle all strife through "the constraint of the clearly recognized
> way of fate." Therefore: "Use your fate, do not strive against it!"[4]

Appropriately, Njord's gemstone is obsidian, philiologically related
to *obstacle, obstruction, obstinacy,* and so forth. It also signifies scarcity
or absence. Our possibilities seem foiled, bound, or hindered. Often, we
ourselves are to blame, so Njord counsels honest introspection and then
the courage needed to "do right and fear no one."

Interestingly, Njord's place in the Norse zodiac is Noatun, his under-
sea palace, and he appropriately corresponds to Pisces, the Fish, which
begins February 19 and concludes on March 20, the vernal equinox,
which happens to be Njord's feast day. The intertwining and inflection
of these relationships reveal the thematic validity of this rune and its
god, a point underscored again by Njord's color, sea blue.

13

Iduna
Gatherer of Golden Apples

The Norse gods were not themselves immortal, but depended for their eternal existence on golden apples that grew from the uppermost branches of Yggdrasil, the Tree of Life. The fruit could be cultivated only by the purest in heart—a forbidding requirement, because all the gods, including Odin, the king of heaven, had at some time or other compromised their divinity, even if for the noblest of causes. In any case, their only exception was a very special Asynir known, not surprisingly, as the Renewing One, Iduna (see color plate 5). The apples of immortality would respond to her pure white hand alone. Before all others, they instantly withered away. So each morning, Iduna went with her basket to the Tree of Life, and there she gathered the special fruits. She served these to the Aesir, Asynir, and Vanir as part of their daily breakfast, for they were the means by which the gods and goddesses shone in vibrant good health throughout time.

While all the world was aware that they feasted on some kind of unique food that gave them eternal youth, only Iduna knew where the golden apples grew. Because of her privileged knowledge, she was the object of numerous conspiracies hatched by the dwarfish and gigantic enemies of the gods. Odin was well aware of these plots, and made certain that both Iduna and her apples were well protected. But he was outwitted, betrayed by one of his own, Loki, the trickster god, who had fallen into trouble with a powerful giant by the name of Thjazi.

Loki had pawned his freedom by promising to deliver Iduna and her apples to Jotunheim. Having never been allowed to taste them, they meant nothing to him, so meeting Thjazi's requirement was no personal loss. Iduna had just picked her daily basketful of fruits and was on her way to serve them to her fellow immortals when Loki breathlessly approached her with supposedly important news.

"A miracle has happened," he exclaimed, "a *great* miracle!" Having won her attention, he told her that another Tree of Life had sprouted overnight just outside the gates of Asgard. "Most remarkable of all," he lied, "it is blossoming with golden apples of eternal youth that are far more beautiful than these relatively pathetic samples you have there." Of course, she demanded to be shown this competitive wonder at once. "Please bring your apples," he suggested shrewdly, "for the sake of comparison. I may have been mistaken, and yours are perhaps still the best in Creation."

"We shall see," Iduna promised, and both marched out of Asgard, while the gods waited in vain for their morning meal of immortality.

Once beyond the shelter of the main gate, she demanded to be shown the other Tree of Life. Instead, Loki suddenly bound and gagged her, threw her over his shoulder, and hiked off with the desired basket of golden apples in the direction of Thrymheim, the giants' grim castle in Jotunheim. He arrived several days later to a mocking if hearty welcome.

"Your ransom is paid," bellowed Thjazi. "Now, get out of here and go hide somewhere, because the giants are about to inherit the earth!" With that, he popped one of the apples into his mouth whole. "One a day keeps the Aesir away!" he laughed, much to Iduna's horror.

Loki fled the giant's dark, immense hall, glad to have been freed from his obligation to such a despicable monster.

Meanwhile, the gods and goddess of Asgard began to wither away. Age, so long postponed, rapidly reclaimed its due, as beauty drained from the faces of the Asynir. Heimdall scarcely had breath enough left to blow his warning Gjallarhorn, and Thor almost lacked strength to lift his war hammer, Mjollnir. Worst of all, Odin's wisdom was fading, so Aesir, Asynir, and Vanir were without effective leadership. Was this the Twilight of the Gods prophesied by Earth Mother? Into their terminal condition, Loki, who was responsible for the calamity, suddenly appeared. He had come straight from Jotunheim, and he confessed his crime. The Trickster was genuinely contrite, less for the wrong that had been done to Iduna and her fellow deities than for fear of Thjazi's intention to conquer the world.

Yet Loki had a plan to undo the evil he had done. "Mardal-Freya," he begged, "lend me your falcon cape! In it, I will fly back to Jotunheim, save Iduna, and return her to Asgard." Too weak to argue, the fading goddess of love gave him her flying cloak of falcon feathers. He wrapped himself in it and was instantly transformed into the appearance of a swift bird of prey that bolted into the sky toward Thrymheim.

He arrived shortly in the land of the giants and circled around the gaunt fortress until he spied hardly more than the slit of a window. He guessed correctly that it belonged to the cell where Iduna was being held captive, and he dived inside. She was sleeping on the hay-strewn stone floor when he cautiously awakened her. "Iduna, it's me, Loki, come to save you!"

"How is that possible," she stirred, "now that you're only a bird?"

In answer, he used his shapeshifting powers to change her into a nut, and, gently grasping her in his talons, flew out the window. Thjazi, although a giant, was no fool. He caught sight of the daring escape and guessed what had happened. He, too, was a master shapeshifter, and he transformed himself into a huge, black eagle. Loki flew as fast as Mardal-Freya's falcon cloak could carry him, but Thjazi's more powerful wings gave the giant greater speed.

Heimdall, the Watcher who sees all things, sounded the alarm with virtually his last strength, and the gods struggled to roll barrels of oil to the highest ramparts of Asgard, as Kvasir stood ready with his torch. At last, even with their diminished eyesight, they could make out two dots in the sky heading their way. The larger one in pursuit was closing in on the smaller bird. The falcon just crossed over the battlements when Kvasir dropped his torch into the hastily spilled pools of spreading oil. Suddenly, rising skyward, there shot a wall of flame from which the eagle fell, its black feathers smoldering. The bird shuddered, then enlarged suddenly into the colossal form of a sprawled giant. Thjazi was dead.

An exhausted Loki cast off the enchanted falcon cape and presented Odin, now a feeble old man, with the nut. "Here's your salvation," he said. In explanation, he changed Iduna back into her original form, and all the other gods and goddesses gathered around to welcome home the blessed goddess. She was appalled at their aged condition and set out at once for the secret Yggdrasil branch. It blossomed in anticipation of her arrival, the golden apples falling of their own accord into her basket. These she hurriedly brought to the wizened Aesir, Asynir, and Vanir. After a few bites, their wrinkles disappeared into the smooth, rosy complexion of robust health. Thor's strength and vigor returned. Odin, standing erect again, no longer leaned on his staff, but instead commanded it. Asgard rang once more with the revelry of restored youth.

Iduna's rune, as her myth dramatizes, involves the cessation of activity, static conditions, an end to progress or development, inertia, entropy, a diminution of energy, a cooling trend. Its appearance cautions us to refrain from making any immediate decisions. She warns us to avoid trouble by refusing to confront it on something other than our own terms. We should wait until more favorable circumstances arise. Putting a positive spin on the sign, McVan states, "it represents drawing into the center of one's being, giving calm in times of strife."[1]

Iduna's color, gold, derives from the life-giving apples she tends.

Her gemstone is the diamond, because it symbolizes her purity. The common Aryan heritage of her significance is demonstrated in the Hindu Kshatriya diamond, which was believed to prevent the approach of old age.[2] Astrologically, the Iduna rune corresponds to Taurus, April 21 to May 20, when it is known as Thrymheim, the name of the giant's castle where she was imprisoned until freed by Loki.

14

Jordegumma
The Old Woman of the Earth

Following long voyages from Sweden's faraway coasts, the members of two different expeditions, unknown to each other, happened to arrive separately but simultaneously on the same eastern shores of Greenland. Both peoples were surprised not only because of their coincidental meeting, but more especially by the cold, hard ground beneath their feet. "We were led to believe that this place would live up to its name," they complained, "but there is nothing green around here. It may be wise to leave now, before the winter overtakes us. But if we return to Scandia, our investment will be lost, and everyone will laugh at us for fools."

So, despite their disappointment, they decided to stay and make the best of their new home. After fairly dividing up the land among themselves, they tried to make a living from the rocky soil—but simply clearing the fields was the most difficult work they had ever encountered. Yet the chief of one tribe told his people they possessed an advantage over their neighbors. For the first time, he revealed his identity as a high priest of the goddess Jordegumma. "She is Earth Mother Erda's generous daughter, the Old Woman of the Earth, the spirit of natural abundance," he explained. "This place is cold and barren because she has never been honored here. We are the first in this part of Greenland. No one was here before us to show her reverence. Yet we can be rich if only we pay her proper homage." Now the priest was a very persuasive man, and desperation had made his people receptive to religious fanaticism. At his urging, they spent many weeks raising an elaborate shrine to Jordegumma, while their neighbors were busily engaged in the backbreaking work of farming.

When the building was complete, the priest gathered his people inside. "Kinsmen, I have great news," he exclaimed. "Jordegumma appeared to me in a dream last night," and his congregation gasped in religious awe. "She told me that all Asgard thanks you for constructing this beautiful shrine. Your labors will soon be blessed with tremendous wealth—and no further work is required of you. While others slave to survive, you do not need to plow, because a rich harvest is about to descend on you from heaven." His audience was ecstatic with this promise, and all previous regrets about sailing to Greenland were forgotten.

"There is just one thing more we need before Jordegumma will consent to shower us with abundance," he said. "Despite the excellence of this shrine, it lacks a suitable image of the goddess. The only one acceptable to her, she told me last night, may be found in Sweden. She commanded me to go there personally, obtain the proper wooden statue, and bring it back here. Once I have set it up in the center of our shrine, her promise will be fulfilled, and we will be the lords of Greenland!"

At the eloquent urging of the priest, everyone present freely gave him numerous gold and silver coins—all they had, in fact—in order to purchase the required carving. They saw him off early the next morning, wishing him a safe voyage and speedy return, as his ship carried him over the eastern sea.

Members of the other tribe expressed admiration for the fine building but wondered how their neighbors could afford the time to undertake such an elaborate project when coaxing a living from the flinty soil was an all-consuming endeavor.

"Oh, we do not have to work as you do," they answered. "Jordegumma will provide," and they entered their new shrine to pray for the success of the devout priest. For the rest of that spring and throughout the summer, they did little else, confident that the goddess would reward their piety. With the onset of fall, however, and sign of neither the Old Woman of the Earth nor the priest, they began to worry about the future. Their concerns were, of course, aggravated by rapidly dwindling supplies. Trusting so completely as they did in the generosity of heaven, they had not bothered to work the land or fish in the surrounding waters.

"What if the priest never comes back?" some began to wonder. "Maybe he was lost in a storm at sea?" In truth, the man had safely arrived in Sweden, where he purchased a fine house with the money collected from his trusting followers after sadly reporting that he was the last survivor of the Greenland colony. Every colonist had died in a famine, he explained, and wept.

Although the Greenlanders were unaware of his treachery, terrifying were the first gusts of a winter they knew they could not survive without charity. Their hardworking neighbors had been blessed with a modest harvest. It was to them now that the mortified settlers appealed for help, promising to repay their assistance amply the next year. Their less religious kinsfolk did not begrudge them assistance, and these shared equally all they possessed in food, shelter, and clothing in order to see their neighbors through the winter. Grateful for the kindness extended to them and chagrined at the dire consequences of their foolishness, the duped settlers vowed to tear down the shrine for Jordegumma on which they had wasted building time and energy. For them, it was no longer a sacred place but instead a monument to their own culpability. The timbers would better serve the construction of new homes for themselves and their neighbors.

They did not turn against the goddess, however. Instead, they learned that she rewarded men and women for their hard toil, and not because of prayers or hollow shrines. The only homage she wanted was human energy devoted to helping new life emerge from the land.

Come springtime, the needy settlers were as good as their word.

They aggressively began work, building and farming in a flurry of activity that greatly improved the harvests and living conditions of the colony. The Old Woman of the Earth did indeed bless them with abundance, just as the priest promised—but for reasons he would never have understood.

Jordegumma's rune signifies the reaping of rewards as a consequence of expended effort. She is, after all, a daughter of the Earth Mother, representing the harvest and natural abundance—the prosperity that comes only after we have exerted our hearts, minds, and muscles in honest labor. More than any other deity, she epitomizes the adage "God helps those who help themselves." She also represents what Joseph Campbell defines as "the authentic life"—that is, performing the kind of work that is personally most meaningful to you.[1] That is the effort you will do best, because it comprises the tasks for which you are most suited. In "following your bliss," you will strive harder for yourself than under any other employer, but the reward of your labors will be a deep sense of satisfaction that is more valuable than any inflated paycheck.

As suggested by her agricultural rhythms, Jordegumma's rune is connnected to all cycles of growth. Not only crops come to fruition, but so does justice. Hence, she is equally concerned with legal matters, including marriage, business deals, and contracts of all kinds. Svensson refers to her sign as "the rune of cyclical return."[2] According to Pennick, "It is the rune of completion at the proper time, for a plentiful harvest can only happen if the right things have been done at the right time."[3] In other words, it represents the natural order of existence. McVan believes that Jordegumma's rune deals with "the progression of the seasons, sowing and reaping, birth, death and rebirth, and the rewards and penalties for one's actions."[4] The birth it implies is not of infants alone but of all new, living things and ideas.

The Jordegumma rune finds its astrological parallel in Capricorn,

December 21 to January 19. To the Norse, this period was Landvidi, the White Land, shared with Aegir and Vidar, gods of the sea and sky. With the Old Woman of the Earth, they form the fundamental levels of our world. Consequently, her color is blue for the heaven above and the ocean beneath. Agate is her gemstone for its association with health and longevity, components of a successful life cycle.

15

Eir

Wolf Mother

At the end of a particularly devastating war, the lands of a vanquished people were occupied by brutal conquerors. Not content with victory, they first indulged in murder and rape, then reduced the survivors to virtual slave status. As a terrible consequence of these events, the light of liberty burned only in the breasts of a small handful of unbowed patriots. They called themselves Ulfheonar, or Wolfskins, a secret band of warriors who disguised themselves in lupine masks during raids on the enemy.

Geri was a young member of this underground movement, and he had special cause to hate the man installed by the conquerors as their puppet chief. In cooperating with the occupiers, Hunding had betrayed his own people, and he was subsequently condemned in the secret counsels of the Ulfheonar as a collaborator marked for death. The traitor was headquartered in a stone fortress, where Geri's new wife, Feri, suffered and wept in a dank, underground prison. She was being used as bait to lure the elusive Wolfskins into a trap, but they were more daring and cunning than Hunding gave them credit for.

Late one night, while he and his lackeys were carousing with their foreign benefactors, Geri stole past the half-drunk guards, through the castle, and down into the fetid dungeon. There he found his wife dying of grief and abuse. To her, his appearance in her lightless cell was like a miraculous vision, but he cautioned her to be brave and wait with him quietly in the darkness for a little while longer. In due course, they could hear the inebriated Hunding stumble alone toward the prison door. It opened, and he bawled, "Tonight's your lucky night, Feri! I am your husband until dawn!" With that, Geri flung himself at the traitor and stabbed him to death. Hunding gave an unexpected shout of mixed agony and terror before collapsing in a bloody heap of flesh onto the cold, stone floor.

The alarm had been sounded with his dying shriek, however, and husband and wife barely escaped in the midst of the resultant chaos. Closely pursued, they ran for their lives into the forest. Soon, the sound of enemy hunting horns seemed to encircle them. They were surrounded, with no way out. The pair was panicked and exhausted.

"Eir!" Geri called out to the goddess of his humiliated people. "Save us!"

The soldiers were keen to avenge Hunding's execution, and their captain ran on ahead of his men, anxious to take Geri and Feri himself, thereby winning the plaudits of his alien overlords. He disappeared into the thick foliage, but only a few moments later, his bloodcurdling screams froze the guardsmen in their tracks. They recovered their composure after an uncertain pause, then rushed forward through the dense forest growth, which eventually opened into a clearing. There, a great yew stood apart from the other trees. On its trunk was deeply cut, as though with fingers of flame, the goddess Eir's rune—a vertical line with angled hooks at either end. Resin, like red blood and poisonous to the touch, streamed from the wound and filled the three strokes of the symbol. Beneath her portentous sign, at the base of the bleeding yew, lay the crumpled corpse of the soldiers' captain, his throat torn out by some inconceivably powerful force.

"Look there!" one of the guards yelled, and some of them caught the fleeting glimpse of a pair of wolves vanishing into the undergrowth. The soldiers did not pursue them.

In the years that followed, Geri and Feri retained their wolf shape. They raised litters of true Ulfheonar to harass and terrify the enemy. How long the struggle for liberty would last, no one knew—but no freedeom fighters doubted its victorious climax, however far in the future it might be.

In the course of time, the devoted Geri and Feri grew old and were near death when Eir appeared to them a second time. Now she escorted them from Midgard, with its ceaseless human conflicts, to the abode of the gods. In Asgard, Odin so admired the pair that he kept them as his own private companions. Thereafter, whenever he sat on his high throne overlooking the world, both were at his feet, and during All-Father's wild rides across the sky on his mighty horse, Geri and Feri ran swiftly and loyally alongside him, ferociously barking and snarling at all tyrants and traitors below.

Eir means "care for" or "save." Eir's rune is protective and signifies the warding off of difficulties or threats. It means that we are shielded from those opposing forces that strive to deflect us from the attainment of goals that are beneficial, just, and reasonable. If we aim at a good target, we are sure to hit it. Like the Ulfheonar, our tactics must remain flexible but steeled by iron determination. Overpowering obstacles may be skirted or outmaneuvered before an attack is renewed. With the correct strategy, escape from or avoidance of any threat or difficulty is assured, and we will have the endurance to see our struggle through.

McVan points out that, paralleling the Ulfheonar, "this rune contains the mystery of life and death. . . ."[1] Indeed, Pennick refers to it as "the death rune."[2] Although our situation may seem bleak at a certain time, the appearance of this glyph indicates that circumstances are about to change for the better. Delays might forestall immediate success, but setbacks are temporary. Eir counsels that they may be overcome with grit, foresight, and decisive action.

She also has a strong mystical dimension. There is a certain immediacy in her willingness to connect mortals and spiritual power in the form of meaningful coincidences or a transformational experience. In other words, her rune signifies direct relationships with occult or arcane energies.

Within Capricorn, the goddess belongs to Landvidi, the White Land, from December 21 to January 19. Smokey quartz is her gemstone, because, like the color blue associated with Eir, it is synonymous with mysticism.

16

Perchta
Keeper of Secrets

Odin and Loki were wandering together throughout Midgard in search of adventure when they came upon an otter consuming immense quantities of salmon at the edge of a waterfall. Now this was no ordinary otter; he was the size of a hay barn.

"If I can kill that prodigious beast," Loki said, "its meat and pelt will feed and clothe all the Aesir and Asynir throughout eternity."

Odin laughed in assent as his companion seized a sharp rock and hurled it with such force and accuracy at the monster that it instantly fell over dead. Almost as suddenly, the giant Hreidmar appeared as though out of nowhere.

"My son," he cried, "my son! Who has murdered you?"

"How can that be?" mused Odin. "How could someone like yourself have an otter for offspring?"

"Well, he certainly was a *giant* otter," commented Loki, and both gods broke into uncontrollable laughter.

"He shapeshifted himself," Hreidmar tearfully explained, "all the better to eat more salmon. Now he has come to such a sad end!"

Overhearing their father's grief, Hreidmar's oafish sons, Fasolt and Fafner, hurried to join him. "This is no laughing matter," Fasolt angrily scolded Odin. "Our brother has been killed. By the very runes you yourself carved on that staff you carry and by which you have ordered the entire universe, you must ransom your lives or lose them! Defy the law, and the Ragnarok will swoop down to consume your fair family."

All-Father knew Fasolt spoke the truth, and so he promised to pay compensation for the dead giant: "What is the penalty?"

The giants conferred among themselves, and thought of a ransom that was too steep for even the gods to pay so that Odin and Loki could be legally executed. "We have decided," Fafner announced: "Your lives will be redeemed on the receipt of enough gold to fill completely the corpse of our brother."

"There is not so much gold in the whole world!" Loki exclaimed.

But Odin gestured for him to be silent. "We accept your demand, against which our lives are pawned. I swear it by my rune staff!"

On that pledge, the gods were free, but only on condition that they return with the promised gold. When they were far enough away from the giants, Loki wondered why All-Father agreed to such an impossible bargain. "They could have rightfully killed us then and there," Odin explained. "Besides, I have heard rumors. . . . We must go to the White Lady to learn more."

The two gods traveled far—to the ends of Midgard, where ceaseless, freezing winds made all human habitation impossible. At the foot of a great mountain, they came upon a broad opening in the rock face. Odin stood at its threshold, his voice echoing throughout its stony chambers: "Wake up, Perchta!" he called into the cave. "From your long sleep, I summon you! Perchta, eternal spirit, from your depths, I conjure you! I am your awakener. All-knowing, wise Perchta, awake!"

As he uttered this incantation, a bluish haze glowed faintly in the otherwise dark recess. The mist gradually became an incandescent cloud of azure light into which the form of a woman arose. "Who disturbs my sleep with such irresistible power?" she spoke as though in a trance, her eyes closed. Her hair was as wild as tangled tree roots, but she wore a mantle of pure white snow about her shoulders.

"Only I, All-Father, am strong enough to call you."

"Why have you done so?" she asked wearily. "Let me sleep!"

"You are the All-Knower, wiser than Mimir, owner of the well of knowledge."

"For which he shall lose his head, as you have lost your eye," she muttered. "What price wisdom now?"

"My life is the price! I need gold enough to fill the body of Hreidmar's son as ransom for the boy's death, else I forfeit not only myself but also the universe."

Perchta was silent a long while as though dreaming, her eyes still shut, before she responded. "Deep under the surface of Midgard is hidden an evil dwarf. For some time now he has enslaved his fellow Niflheimers, forcing them to become miners. They work perpetually and in utmost secrecy, hacking great quantities of gold from deep inside the earth. The piles of glittering metal grow higher and higher under Alberich's whip. With this wealth, he plans someday to buy the mercenary services of all the giants. They are to be his paid dupes for the storming of Asgard. After its destruction, he will rule the world, something his people have been scheming for a long time.

"The dwarf has all the gold you need. Take it. But he also possesses a ring you may not keep. That small circle of gold is the source of Alberich's power over his fellow dwarves. He stole it from the Rhine maidens. To accomplish the theft, he had to forever foreswear love—not a difficult thing for such an unloveable creature. But in so doing, he placed a curse on the ring. Anyone who wears it wields ultimate power, but is doomed. Seize the gold, but avoid the curse, Odin! Return the ring to its rightful if inept guardians!"

Without committing himself to such a request, All-Father thanked Perchta for sharing her secret wisdom, then gently allowed her to sink back into subterranean sleep.

He and Loki straightaway flew down to Niflheim, where they seized Alberich, bound him in chains, and carried him back to Hreidmar, who was still waiting by the side of his dead son with Fasolt and Fafner.

"Summon your people here! Have them bring us all the gold they have mined or, by Odin's staff, you will die most miserably for it!" Loki threatened the cringing dwarf.

Alberich reluctantly muttered a gruff command over the glittering ring on his dirty, crooked finger. The earth opened, and a throng of dwarves pulling wagonloads of gold pushed innumerable bars of the costly metal into the dead otter. Eventually, the body seemed entirely filled, which was lucky for Odin and Loki, because every scrap of gold had been stuffed into the gigantic carcass, now bloated with treasure.

"Wait!" Fasolt commanded the departing Aesir. "Not so fast! You have not paid your ransom. My poor dead brother has not been entirely filled with gold, as you agreed. Look here!" And he showed them a tiny open space in the creature's maw.

"That is easily filled," Odin said. He grabbed Alberich and wrestled the little circle of gold from his finger. "Here, that should do it," as he placed the cursed ring inside the otter's mouth.

The gods won more than freedom. Their enemies destroyed each other, just as Perchta had foreseen. Hreidmar claimed the ring, but subsequently became the victim of parricide at the hands of Fasolt. He, too, was murdered soon after by his brother, who turned himself into a loathsome dragon, all the better to guard the otter-filled treasure. Fafner, too, died violently, a hero's swordblade in his breast. And so the ring's curse went from victim to victim, until it helped bring about the end of the world.

Perchta is concerned with mysteries of all kinds—occult, hidden things; buried or concealed valuables; the unknown. The appearance of her rune means that a secret is about to be disclosed, an undiscovered or suppressed truth revealed. Something lost is about to be found. It also promises new opportunities. The energies associated with her are almost invariably positive, although the information revealed may be disturbing. Her rune suggests that memories, feelings, and urges that are unintentionally or deliberately forgotten are surfacing for good or ill. There is a difference between the thrill or satisfaction of discovery and the shock or embarrassment of exposure. Disclosure may be public or private, and it may possibly be traumatic. Her rune, after all, represents the mouth of a cave, such as the one from which Perchta appeared to Odin. It signifies things that are open or opening.

On a material level, the Perchta rune can herald unexpected financial gains, even unearned income—such as an inheritance, a lucky gambling streak, the winning of monetary prizes, great wealth. Yet, at the time of its appearance, it cautions against making investments or granting loans, especially if a friend is involved.

The Perchta rune is theurgic: It is the manipulation of spiritual power in the material world. McVan writes that the glyph represents "intellectual knowledge and divination."[1] He is seconded by Pennick, who believes that "it gives us access both to the inner secrets of the human world and also to the inner-workings of nature. It empowers us with the ability to distinguish things of value from those that are worthless . . . it exposes things that previously were concealed, turning potential into physical reality."[2] Psychometry, psychokinesis, remote viewing, and all manner of psychic abilities are open to the person who draws her glyph—but, like the Niflheim ring's curse, such abilities are to be employed wisely and fairly, or the consequences of abuse may be particularly unpleasant.

As the White Lady, it is only fitting that Perchta belongs to the White Land of Landvidi, the Norse equivalent of Capricorn, December 21—the winter solstice—to January 19. Her gemstone, white onyx, likewise symbolizes the purity of her wisdom. This is further enhanced by her color, black, signifying mystery.

17

Odin

All-Father

After Odin finished building the cosmos, he was ambitious to attain greater wisdom and power. Indeed, both go together. For this purpose, he created two ravens, Hugin and Munin, Thought and Memory. Each morning, as he sat on his high throne from which he surveyed the various levels of existence spread out before him, they would perch on his shoulders and repeat into his ears all the gossip they had learned. He was therefore kept abreast of everything that went on around the world.

One morning, Hugin told Odin of an ancient creature, Mimir, who had survived the Great Flood and still lived alone at the far edge of Jotunheim, realm of the hostile giants. There he guarded a remote spring that granted deep wisdom to anyone who drank from it. "I must taste its waters," Odin decided, and he straightaway followed Hugin for many days to Mimir's abode. It was a simple, undecorated hut before which the antediluvian giant rested in a sprawling chair beside his crudely made well of rough stone.

"So, Odin," Mimir said while All-Father was still a few paces away, "you've come to enjoy my spring at last. You did not waste any time."

"Mimir, I can see you have been drinking from your own well. How else would you have known all about me? Yes, I mean to have its waters myself. I need wisdom to govern the world."

"If you were truly wise," Mimir interrupted, "you would not bother.

But you seem determined to pursue your fate. You may drink from my well. Drink deeply. There is a charge for the service, however."

"I expected as much. Name your price!"

"It is costly, but then, so is wisdom. You must first tear out one of your eyes with your own hand. That done, you may have your fill. If you do not make this payment, however, when you leave this place, you will never be able to return for a second chance. Now you know why no one drinks from Mimir's well!"

Odin paused. What the giant demanded was a fearful thing. Truly, such a self-sacrifice had never before been asked or made. Yet if he lost his nerve now and departed as unwise as he had come, his ascendency over the other gods might be called into question. Moreover, he knew he lacked the knowledge to order the universe as he should. His instinctive defiance of obstacles, no matter how apparently insuperable, rose in his veins like hay fire.

"I'll have my drink," Odin declared. "Here is the payment you require!" And with neither another moment's hesitation nor a single groan, the king of the Aesir gouged out his left eye from its socket. He presented it to the giant, who immediately deposited it in a small, golden cask filled with similarly grisly momentos, then he handed Odin a clean, wet towel with which to wash his bloody face.

"You have paid the price, Burri's son! Now take your drink. You have earned it."

Odin stood at the edge of the well, gazing into its crystal-clear depths with his remaining eye, then he took a nearby wooden pail by its handle and dipped it full into the spring. Putting it to his lips, he drank long and deeply to its dregs. As he did so, his thoughts began to assume the same clarity as the water. It was as though his mind was bathed in sunshine. His perspective seemed magnified a thousandfold.

"Now that you have what you have come for," Mimir warned him, "do not imagine you have all or even enough. What you obtain henceforward you must win by yourself. Of wisdom, no one can ever have too much, and there are many pitfalls to be avoided."

He was right, because not even Mimir, for all the knowledge that filled his head, could keep his head on his shoulders: he later fell into the hands of his enemies, who decapitated him. Just as the god had lost an eye for wisdom, the giant lost his head—but even this event did not entirely disturb Odin, because hearing of old Mimir's misfortune, he acquired the severed head. Despite its disembodied condition, it continued to give good advice when consulted, especially in trying times, of which many came, like flocks of gathering birds of prey.

All-Father meanwhile continued to grow in power and understanding, but even he was unable to avoid the Twilight of the Gods that would inevitably overwhelm him and his universe. That Day of Doom was yet far off in the future, however. For now, the awful loss of his eye seemed almost small payment for the potent wonder that filled his mind and coursed through his whole being.

"Give me the other eye," cried Mimir, "and take another drink."

"Ha! A blind king of the world! He would make for a fine ruler, wouldn't he?"

"True," Mimir said seriously, "you would no longer be king, but you would be wiser. You have knowledge now to govern but not yet enough to know that there are greater things even than that kind of power." Odin considered taking out his other eye, but the prospect made him shudder.

Mimir continued with mystical confidentiality: "To behold the real treasures within, we must forever avert our gaze from the illusion of mere phenomena. Are you brave enough for that?"

"You cannot tempt me to blindness," Odin laughed good-naturedly, then he thanked Mimir for the offer of the drink. "A dead eye. What's that good for?"

"Your eye?" Mimir patted the golden cask's locked lid. "Oh, that. Nothing in itself beyond a souvenir of self-sacrifice for something greater than oneself." Later, after the god departed, Mimir took the eye from its golden receptacle and tossed it into the well. Perhaps its ghastly appearance there would act as a further deterrent to other would-be wise men.

Somewhere along his homeward journey, Odin struck off a branch of

Yggdrasil to use as a walking staff. Sitting on the verdant carpet of moss in the cool shade of the World Tree, he unsheathed his dagger and began paring off the twigs. As is common among whittlers everywhere, his thoughts ran free. With Mimir's water still fresh in his throat, a new awareness crowded his consciousness and was bursting for expression. His large hands spoke for his seething mind, creating carved signs and symbols for the new concepts that percolated within him. These were the first runes, suffused with his spirit and the powers they represented. He marveled; it was almost as though they had carved themselves, and he proudly examined his uniquely decorated walking stick. Then he resumed his journey.

Days later, shortly before the other dwellers in Asgard could actually see him, they saw the aura of his newfound wisdom approaching from afar, glowing like a rainbow after summer thunderstorms. When he finally arrived, they were amazed by his transformation and bent down to admire the strange runes freshly carved in the staff. As they reverently fingered each one, Odin realized with something of a shock that the twenty-four glyphs corresponded to the same number of gods and goddesses.

"Choose one for yourselves," he offered his fellow deities, "and imbue it with your own energies."

They did so, and the simple walking staff suddenly became a great wand of unprecedented potency. Its possession made him the master of the universe. Only after these things did Frija, his magnificent wife, learn that her husband had lost his left eye when she brushed aside the long lock of hair he used to conceal the recent disfigurement. She screamed in horror, and he needed all his newly won understanding to calm her distress. Balder, the god of beauty, fetched him a simple leather eye patch to wear, but Thor stood by, holding a long, sharp lance point made of solid iron.

"Here, this will make your walking staff into something greater. The most potent scepters are always spears." It fit with perfect snugness, and henceforward Odin wielded his rune-carved rod over the destinies of gods and men.

As Wotan, Odin's name derives from the German *wut,* "to rage," and defines his identification with the dynamic forces of creation and destruction over which he has almost ultimate power. Since prehistoric times, he has also been known as Vodan and Votan to the Indo-European peoples of northern Europe. Odin is chief deity of Asgard—the great culture creator and bearer—the one who invented and brought to humankind the civilizing gifts of poetry, literacy, wisdom, the arts, law, and medicine.

Sometimes, Odin appears among mortals dressed in the great cloak and large, slouch hat of a traveler, and his spear is made to resemble a walking stick. At such times, he is the Wanderer who roams Midgard for personal adventure and to learn firsthand how goes the world. He is the most potent sorcerer: secret magic enables his godhood and brings supernatural power to anyone with whom he shares some of his runic mysteries. As such, he is the god of wisdom. Together with Thor and Ullr, Odin oversees Breidablikk, the Broad Gleaming, from July 21 to August 21, a period corresponding to the zodiacal Leo. The color of his rune is deep purple for the royal robe worn by the king of the Aesir. His is called the god rune, signifying Odin's divine primacy.

In northern Europe, the constellation of the Great Bear is known instead as Odin's Wain ("wagon" or "cart"). Our Wednesday is a contraction of Woden's Day. His rune relates to Odin, also known as Galdrafoedhur, "Father of Incantation."[1] McVan, too, connects it with All-Father: "[T]his rune stands for wisdom and divine inspiration. Consciousness, intelligence, poetry, magic, ecstasy and order. . . . It is the wisdom of ancestral memory and that 'small voice within.'" It is "instrumental in the creation of mankind. It is the rune which works magnetic and/or hypnotic speech."[2] Svensson similarly associates it with communication, writing, speaking, and poetry—all leading qualities of the god.[3]

Guido von List likewise defines it as "spiritual power working through speech."[4] Peschel writes that the Odin rune represents helpful advice, the acquisition of wisdom, eloquence, and the power of the spoken word.[5] Its inverse indicates the presence of dishonesty, lies, half truths, deceitful propaganda—false speech.

18

Sif

The Golden-Haired

The Gibichungs had dwelled peacefully in their ancestral lands along the western banks of the Oder River for unknown generations. Though preferring farming to war, they nonetheless were quite capable of defending themselves from outside raiders and had successfully repelled many attacks in the history of their country. There came a time, however, when even their matchless courage seemed insufficient to stem a new threat from the east. A host of Mongolian horsemen was amassing for an invasion that outnumbered the defenders ten to one. Chances of defeating such an overwhelming force did not appear positive.

The tribal *voelva,* a respected seeress with a reputation for accuracy, was consulted by Gibichung military commanders. Spreading a rune cast for divine guidance in their difficult crisis, she held up a pebble emblazoned with the sign of a single lightning bolt. "What does it mean? Will Thor help us?" they questioned her.

"No," she disappointed them. "This generation of Gibichungs is too selfish and greedy. He does not believe we deserve to survive."

"Is there nothing we can do to save ourselves?"

"Well, perhaps."

"Tell us, and no matter what heaven asks, we will do it!"

"Thor pays us no attention, but an offering to his beloved wife may return his favor."

"What might that offering be?"

"Burn your harvests. Pray when you do so that the ripe wheat is to honor Sif, the golden-haired. Maybe then she will intercede for you with her husband."

The military commanders were aghast. "Even if we defeated the enemy," they cried, "we would soon after die of starvation if we destroyed our crops."

"Do it," the voelva snapped impatiently, "or face the inevitable!"

They consulted in earnest among themselves and agreed that their people had grown somewhat degenerate. But to burn all their food? That seemed suicidal. Princes, nobles, and common people were told of the voelva's rune cast. To a man and woman, all urged the immolation of the harvests they had worked so long and hard to bring forth.

"What is wealth without life?" they wondered. "Let us trust the gods who have been good to us for so long!"

After sunset that very evening, in a special ceremony conducted by the voelva, stacks of wheat were gathered on the fields, then these were set alight. Their flames roared toward the stars, turning night into day, but the Gibichungs were not sorrowful. They gave vent to loud battle cries, the most defiant ever heard, and trumpeted their *lurs*—war horns—as the sacrifice to Sif blazed like a comet come to Earth.

All this was secretly observed from the other side of the Oder River by a Mongolian scout. His report reached the khan himself. After hearing it, the leader decided to attack the Gibichungs at once. He would take them unawares, he explained to his generals, because they were obviously in the midst of celebrating some kind of agricultural festival. "We'll move against them in the morning."

Meanwhile, the Gibichungs planned that very same day to pull down the two big bridges that spanned the Oder, thereby forcing the enemy to cross in boats that might be picked off by the defending archers. The Mongols, however, possessed many more soldiers than the Gibichungs had arrows. At most, destroying the bridges would gain them time for a vigorous defense that would at least cost the enemy dearly.

Plate 1.
Frija, the Queen of Heaven

Plate 2.
Thor, the Protector

Plate 3.
Ran, Goddess of the Sea

Plate 4.
Aegir, the Oceanic God

Plate 5.
Iduna, Gatherer of Golden Apples

Plate 6.
Kvasir, the Divine Inspirer

Plate 7.
Ostara, Goddess
of Spring

Plate 8.
Vidar, Conqueror of Doom

They believed that because to run away meant slow death by starvation, they might as well stay and fight to be killed more quickly.

But they did not expect the invasion for another several days—thus they were horrified when the enormous horde of Mongolians already assembled on the far bank of the river began crossing its two undestroyed bridges. Alarms sounded, and the defenders poured out of their homes, many still in the process of pulling on armor, just as the first wave of Mongolians stormed on to the western bank. Desperation, superior skill, and finer weapons made the Gibichungs better fighters, and the mounds of dead invaders rose on the blood-slick battleground. Still the khan, who kept well to the rear on the other side of the river, had numbers on his side. He opened the floodgates of his reserves, and they cascaded across the bridges toward the west.

Unobserved by either side, storm clouds were gathering overhead, and occasional thunder rumbled from the sky. The combatants were too busily engaged in mutual slaughter to notice. Both bridges bulged with Mongolian reinforcements that pushed their way toward the Gibichungs, who strained to the breaking point under pressure of the enemy's growing numerical strength. At the moment when collapse of the Gibichungs seemed imminent, a blinding flash of forked lightning exploded from the darkening sky, along with deafening thunder claps. The twin-pronged bolt struck both bridges simultaneously, entirely electrocuting the crowds of iron-armored soldiers who were trying to cross. They and their horses were killed by the thousands where they stood, their blackened corpses smoldering like heaps of burned meat.

The stunned khan gradually regained his senses, then ordered fresh reserves to resume the attack. But his troops refused to move. They fell prostrate before the bridges of death and prayed to heaven for mercy. Seizing the moment, the Gibichungs rallied and, with renewed ferocity, counterattacked the enemy stranded on the western side of the Oder. The Mongolians, however, were emotionally off-balanced by the divinely inspired annihilation on the bridges. They defended themselves halfheartedly, for all their numbers, and gradually began laying down their arms. The survivors were allowed to make their way back over the bridges among the ghastly, charred remains of their comrades. The kahn spoke not a word to these returning warriors, but waved them compassionately back into the ranks of his silent army. He ordered its about-face, and the Mongolian hordes returned in despair to the wild regions of their homeland beyond the Ural Mountains.

The exhausted Gibichungs could not believe their good fortune. Sif's rune, chosen by the voelva the previous day, had come to life in a most potent form and had turned the tide of battle at its most crucial moment. Nor would victory bring the Gibichungs the starvation they feared. Numerous enemy supply wagons had been captured. The abundance of preserved food they carried, enough to feed an army, would see the Gibichungs through the winter.

Sif's lightning bolt rune embodies decisive action. Like her, its appearance means that success will come if undertaken with a brave heart and good intention. It signifies victory from any angle, featuring no negative aspects, unlike most of the other runes. But it does not automatically guarantee success. We must be willing to act and struggle for what we want. If we struggle to the best of our abilities, victory is promised us. Then again, it may not come in the shape we anticipate. However we achieve it, though, the spoils of victorious action belong to us.

As Guido von List points out, the profound antiquity of the Sif rune echoes in the greeting "Sal und Sig!" (Sal[vation] and Victory!), used by the tribal Indo-European peoples five thousand years ago, when they stormed out of their primeval homelands in what are now the steppes of central Russia. *Sal* also implied health and the all-conquering sun, revered in Roman times as Sol Invictus.[1] McVan associates this rune with "the sun and the power it radiates. It represents the primal fire that reacts against ice. It is the power of the human will, of victory and success."[2] Svensson writes that it "symbolizes the life force itself."[3] Appropriately, it is associated with the sun stone, an early form of navigational compass that refracted solar rays in such a way as to roughly define north.

The Sif rune, unlike any other sign in the Elder Futhark, powers its own positive aspects or reduces—sometimes even negates—its negative features. Pennick associates it with the astrological Valaheim, corresponding to the House of Aquarius, January 20 to February 18, and equivalent to the old Norse month of Lios-Beri, or, appropriately enough, Light Bringer. Sif's hair is described in the sagas as having been spun from the finest gold, another solar reference associated with the golden wheat harvest.

Her rune personifies strength, vitality, self-confidence, personal power. The victory it achieves is so total that it brings deep satisfaction and a sense of inner peace. Her rune teaches that we must pursue a heroic passage through life, discarding the pointless acquisition of mere material wealth. Sif epitomizes the authentic life spent joyfully fighting for our deepest convictions, "following our bliss." Such a life, regardless of whether the final goal is attained, is victorious in and of itself.

19

Tyr

War God

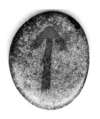

With the completion of Asgard, the gods settled into their sky domain of estates and palaces, where they played with a wolf cub called Fenris. For some time, he was a friendly pup, but he grew steadily in size and strength until even the Aesir were afraid of him. Eventually, the only god brave enough to feed the creature was Tyr, the divine patron of war. Still, the wolf continued to grow, reaching monstrous proportions and filling heaven with his incessant howling. The gods finally had enough. They planned to bind him away in some remote corner of the universe—not an easy task, even for them, because Fenris was now the largest, most dangerous beast in Creation.

Consulting his runes, Odin determined how this was to be done. He sent a commission to Niflheim, ordering the most skilled craftsmen there to forge a chain that could never be broken. The dwarves put their heads together and came up with fetters as unbreakable as they were invisible. They were made from the unseen powers, which are the strongest: the roots of a mountain, the sound of a moving cat, and the breath of a fish.

Odin was skeptical when the Niflheimers showed him the chain, no more than a silken band, but they assured him of its efficacy. "Of course, the only difficulty," they told him, "will be putting it on Asgard's misbehaving pet. But that is your problem, not ours."

Indeed, it was, so the gods had to come up with some kind of a plan. Odin showed Fenris the frail cord, explaining as reassuringly as he could that it was meant to honor, not bind him. But the creature was suspicious and agreed to have it put on him only if someone could be found to place his or her hand inside the wolf's jaws as a pledge that the silken twine was harmless. Tyr stepped forth at once to save his fellow Vanir any embarrassment, and he boldly thrust his left hand into the mouth of the beast as the gods tied Fenris's limbs and neck with the deceptively thin cord. When Fenris moved to test his fetters, he found that he was bound fast after all, and he bit off Tyr's hand before the war god could remove it in time. The wolf raged and strained in his chains, but they held firm and will continue to do so until Ragnarok at the end of the world.

Tyr is the Scandinavian version of an important deity known among earlier Germanic peoples as Tiwaz, from which our Tuesday derives. The Etruscans of twenty-eight centuries ago revered him as Tarchon. Wherever the Aryan tribes spread, he was central to their worship. His image in the form of a red horse nearly an acre in extent (250 feet long by 200 feet high) was cut into the side of Edge Hill, seven miles from Banbury, England. Both names of the locations associated with the ancient bioglyph refer to the war god: Tysoe and Warwickshire. In spring, every Palm Sunday, sixth-century Anglo-Saxons scoured the outline of the figure, which they called Tiw. The precise location of the Vale of the Red Horse is no longer known, because the hill figure was obliterated probably sometime in the late-eighteenth century.

The profound antiquity of Tyr-Tiwaz traces back to *dieus,* the "shining god" held in awe by Indo-European horsemen of seven thousand and more years ago. It was from this primeval dieus that the Greek Zeus and the later German Ziw descended. An *Edda* poem of the Viking age describes how warriors, before entering battle, carved victory runes using Tyr's name.[1] Archaeological evidence supports the old epic. A second-century-BC helmet from Negau, Austria, is inscribed "Teiwa," a variant of Tyr, and spears found in Britain (at Kowel and Holborough, Kent) bear his rune. Accordingly, it forms the first letter of his name in the shape of a spear.

Upright, Tyr's sign guarantees success in any competition and embodies single-mindedness, willpower, and strong motivation. Increases in power or wealth not by mere chance, but through struggle, are signified by Tyr's glyph. It is the emblem of passion and virility—but risk and sacrifice are also involved. We must dare to win. Struggle is the way of the world, and whoever shirks it can never win. Tyr is the god of the lost cause who teaches that fighting for what we believe is victory in itself. It is our participation in the struggle, not its outcome, that is significant. We must look upon opportunities for victory or defeat with an equally indifferent eye. All that matters is that we do our best for what our heart deems most valuable. Tyr's is the rune of combat and willingness for self-sacrifice on behalf of an ideal or for our own defense or conquest. Implicit are the virtues of duty and honor.

Not surprisingly, Tyr's jewel is the bloodstone. His color, as evidenced in his nature and the English hill figure at Warwickshire, is red. He occupies a place in the astrological Noatun, or Pisces, from February 19 to March 20.

Inverted, Tyr means impotence, loss of will, dwindling energy, failure in competitive circumstances, lack of sufficient interest, declining enthusiasm, false expectations that what we want may be achieved with little or no effort. Tyr preaches that prosperity is no one's birthright, but instead must be conquered to be obtained.

20

Balder

The Deathless

Odin and Frija had twin sons. Tragically, Hodur was born blind, but he possessed such an affable heart and cheerful smile that he was universally pitied and beloved. He was quietly devoted to his brother, Balder, whose fair features were matched only by his generous soul. The two were inseparable, and never a cross word passed between them. But Balder, because he lacked his brother's disability, was chosen by All-Father to serve as the divine patron of beauty and art. Nonetheless, he shared as much of his aesthetic duties as possible with Hodur.

Frija so loved Balder that she went to the trouble of extracting an oath from all plants, trees, stones, and metals that they would never bring harm to her son, even if they were fashioned into the most powerful engines of destruction. One plant, however, she overlooked. Small and inconspicuous, it grew not on the ground, but from an oak tree. Thus, the mistletoe was the only thing in all Creation with the potential to hurt Balder.

After Frija presented the protective blessing to her son, he playfully volunteered as a living target, and the other gods enjoyed throwing all manner of weapons at him. Everyone laughed when a spear flung by Tyr, the unerring war god, deflected at right angles in front of Balder. Even Thor's giant-killing hammer bounced away from him as though it had struck an invisible mountain. One after another, the gods delighted in hurling a variety of clubs, axes, and assorted arms at Frija's uniquely shielded son.

While the happy sounds of this unusual entertainment echoed through Asgard, Loki planned to disrupt it in the worst possible way. He had been at odds with heaven before, but his pranks had been more mischievous than serious. For Balder, however, the Trickster nourished a deep-seated hatred born of envy. Among gods, as well as humans, ugliness and evil strive to bring down beauty and goodness. Through his contacts among the elementals of Alfheim, Loki learned of Frija's single oversight, and he had a sharp spear fashioned from mistletoe. With this weapon, he approached Hodur, who was standing outside the crowd of Aesir and Vanir, merrily firing their projectiles at his unassailable brother.

"Why be left out of all the fun?" he asked facetiously. "I will help you. Here, take your turn with this wooden spear!" After placing it in Hodur's hand, Loki carefully positioned him at the proper distance from his brother. Then, taking aim on the blind fellow's behalf, told him to throw with all his strength. To everyone's horror, the shaft struck Balder with great force in the center of his chest. The god of beauty collapsed to the ground, mortally wounded, as Loki made good his escape, if only temporarily. At first, confused and alarmed by the sudden consternation around him, when Hodur learned what had happened, he died instantly of grief. Henceforward, the Norse name for mistletoe was *guidhel,* or "guide to hell."

Odin flew on his horse to the infernal regions of Hela, who had charge over the dead. "Give me back my son!" he pleaded.

"By your own laws carved in holy runes on that staff you carry," she explained, "I am bound to keep him here. But I will make an exception in his case, because he was murdered under the worst treachery and died long before his time: if you can persuade every man and woman in the world to shed tears for Balder, I will release him, and he may return alive to Asgard."

All-Father and the rest of the gods and goddesses immediately got to work, and soon all humankind was weeping for the betrayed god—all but an irascible old woman who bitterly characterized Balder as a pompous fool, an arrogant dandy, and a disgrace to Asgard. "Let him rot forever in Hela's house!" No amount of pleas or threats could change the hag's hard heart, because she was really Loki himself, who had shapeshifted into the appearance of a nasty crone. Poor Balder was forced to remain among the dead.

But the mistletoe with which he had been assassinated possessed a magical quality that not even Loki suspected. It guaranteed, over the course of time, that anyone who had been innocently sacrificed by the plant would eventually gain eternal life. And so it eventually came to pass that after heaven and Earth were destroyed in the Ragnarok, Balder emerged from the ruins of Hela's realm to rule over a new world of light, beauty, and kindness.

Balder's rune presages birth, gestation, and regeneration or rebirth of all kinds—the eternalness of life. "It points clearly to inception, whether of a child, a project or simply an idea," according to Svensson.[1] It is the symbol of fertility and new growth commonly associated with mothers and their offspring. The glyph stands for a favorable outcome, the happy result of plans or endeavors. In metaphysical terms, Balder represents the eternal quality of life that is not destroyed by death, but instead only defined by it. Describing the rune in this context, Guido von List observes, "human life between birth and death means but one day, stands in contrast to this day-in-the-life in human form . . . life is bounded by birth and death. . . ."[2]

Balder's gemstone, jet, simultaneously symbolizes the blackness of death and the soil from which new life springs. His place in the zodiac is Bilskirni, or Lightning, the Norse equivalent of Aries, March 21 (the vernal equinox, significantly enough) to April 20.

Reversed, the Balder rune signals domestic problems and warns of potential trouble in family life. When business or financial questions are at issue, the glyph does not bode well for the immediate future. Whatever successes we might attain in spite of the rune will be temporary.

21

Erda
Earth Mother

Of the nine Valkyries, Bruennhilde was Odin's favorite child. It was with particular bitterness, then, that he stripped her of her godhood by kissing her eyes closed. Out of compassion for a warrior she had tried to shield from death, against Odin's orders, the disobedient daughter had lost her place in Asgard. She fell into a deep sleep from which only the kiss of a mortal hero could awaken her. To prevent all but the most valiant from reaching Bruennhilde, All-Father encircled the high summit of a mountain on which she slept with a ring of otherwise impenetrable fire. In the years that followed, everyone came to know the perpetually burning mountaintop, and all would-be suitors to the ex-Valkyrie were turned away by the intense flames that protected her—all, that is, but Siegfried.

Orphaned as an infant, he had been brought up by a dwarf for strictly ulterior motives. The Niflheimer wanted Siegfried to obtain a golden horde and the ring of ultimate power by slaying Fafner, a giant who guarded this treasure in the guise of a dangerous dragon. That accomplished, the dwarf would poison Siegfried and take possession of the giant's valuables. When the lad came of age, he duly killed Fafner, but then he dispatched the scheming Niflheimer after learning of his murderous intentions. The gold interested him not in the slightest. He kept the ring only as a souvenir of his fight with the dragon. Ignorant of the sleeping Bruennhilde, Siegfried happened upon her blazing enclosure by chance, was drawn toward its mystery and strode through the fire without scorching a single hair. The flames died away, leaving him alone with the prostrate figure dressed in fine armor.

"What a magnificent warrior," he assumed. To his surprise, the figure appeared to be breathing, so he undid the strap on the ornate helmet and visor and was shocked when a mane of bright golden hair cascaded into view. "That is no man!" he exclaimed. Overcome by her matchless beauty, he bent over and kissed her softly on the lips.

Bruennhilde opened her eyes. Staring into Siegfried's innocent face, she knew that he, of all mortal men, must be the best. Their love was at first sight, and they decided to spend the rest of their lives as husband and wife. Both had lost their homes, however, and they could not stay on the barren summit. To complicate their dilemma, rain began to fall, so, at the first opportunity, they sought shelter in a cave down the mountain slope. The spirit of Earth Mother Erda had wordlessly guided their search—but this was no temporary sanctuary from the storm. The interior was tall and deep, and a spring of fresh water ran at the rear. From its entrance the vast, forested valley spread westward toward the far horizon. Bruennhilde and Siegfried could not imagine a more perfectly beautiful location in which to live. Having been cut off from their troubled past, they found a place of new beginnings for them both, but it was the love they shared that formed their true home.

Erda was the Norse Earth Mother, whose daughters Jordegumma and Perchta personified different mystical qualities of the world in much the same way Greek Persephone was the daughter of Demeter. Erda tells of relocation to a new domicile, of finding our dream house. Her rune is often concerned with issues regarding our true home not only in its physical sense but also where the heart is—namely, one's proper place in the world: an environment that nurtures the development of our innermost truths and personal potential to fulfill them. Our real home lies wherever that which we love most dwells. Hence, the Earth Mother sign may apply to particularly cherished interests or those things that give most meaning to our lives.

In marriage, the relationship between a man and woman, more than any other consideration—even those of children—is the true home of husband and wife. Guido von List refers to this glyph as "the marriage-rune," with emphasis on the sacred quality of the bond between the the spouses.[1] McVan declares that it "is a symbol of the ideal man-woman relationship, and thus is the mystery of the lawful marriage."[2] In this spirit, we understand clearly Garman Lord's characterization of Erda's sign as "the better house."[3]

It also implies slow change, like the geological process of continental drift. The implication here is gradual but progressive movement culminating in fundamentally significant shifts or transitions. Suggested too are matters dealing with land, real estate, personal properties, or environmental issues. On an individual level, the rune is assurance of having taken the correct path—the notion that we will eventually reach our desired goal or destination, provided we have the persistence and fortitude to keep pushing onward. The changes foretold here are almost invariably positive occurrences, the happy outcome of processes already known to us.

Reversed, Erda's symbol cautions against pursuing the present objective. The goal—or the means used to reach it—are flawed and must be reexamined. Her inverted rune could mean that we are out of sync with our surroundings and must find those circumstances attuned to our own personality.

The Erda rune's gem is turquoise, a name unknown until the end of the Viking age in the early thirteenth century. Before then, the greenish blue stone was variously referred to as *callais* and a number of other mostly forgotten names. Traditions in various parts of the world claim it has the power to prevent injuries from falls, thereby demonstrating the connection between turquoise and the Earth Mother associated with this rune. The rune's place in the Norse zodiac, Valaheim, or the Halls of Silver, is within Aquarius, from January 28 to February 12, although its color is a brown earth hue.

22

Mardal-Freya
Goddess of Sexual Romance

A young fisherman had the bad luck to live in a small village where men outnumbered women ten to one. Competition for a sweetheart or wife was too much for a poor man like himself, who barely made a living from the indifferent ocean, despite the purity of his heart. Because he worked with the sea on a daily basis, he prayed early one morning for divine help, then tossed into the water a small amethyst, one of his few prized possessions, as a heartfelt sacrifice to the goddess of love. A powerful current suddenly seized the skiff in which he rode. Wondering if he had offended some deity, he held on in terror as his little craft, ignoring all his commands, headed out across the open sea.

His homeland disappeared over the horizon, but the weather was pleasant and the surface of the water calm, and by late afternoon an island came into view. The fisherman's boat continued its progress at high speed toward the unknown shore. The closer he came, the clearer he could make out what appeared to be an agitated crowd of people on the beach. Soon, he heard their urgent shouting, but could not understand them.

Now there was another call, this one a nearby cry for help. The little boat made straight for someone splashing in distress, and the fisherman reached over the side just in time to pull on board a floundering swimmer. He was astonished to see a young woman of exceptional beauty, for all her exhaustion and wild appearance. Overcoming his astonishment, he wrapped her in a blanket, gave her a sip of grog to warm her, then dried her long, golden hair with his shirt.

The skiff, still in the grip of some powerful current, shot straight to shore, beaching itself amid a throng of rejoicing ladies-in-waiting—for the girl he fortuitously plucked from the water was a princess who had ventured out too far while enjoying a swim. Her father, the king, was gratitude itself, and offered anything the fisherman's heart desired. That was, of course, the hand of his daughter, who loved her rescuer less because he had saved her life than for the kind heart she knew beat in his breast. The fisherman was made a prince of the realm, and he married the golden-haired beauty. Many years later, after he ascended to the throne, he was known as the Fisher King, who played the part of a virtuous ruler in numerous stories told long thereafter about the quest for the Holy Grail, which was said to have resided at one time in his own castle. All this had come about through the powerful current Mardal-Freya used to answer his prayer for love.

As testimony to her widespread veneration and its longevity, the goddess Freya had many names and titles. The earliest of these, and therefore the one most appropriately representing her rune in the Elder Futhark, was Mardal, for *marr*, the sea, whose natural abundance she personified. Whether on land or water, she blessed the love affairs of men and women. With her twin brother, Freyr, she ensured human fertility in terms of erotic love and social accord. Appropriately, her rune deals with humankind, Midgard, and human society. Hers is perhaps the closest relationship between the gods and humanity, because she gave her followers a mystery cult known as Sejdr (pronounced "say-ther").

This was an early form of tantric yoga involving altered states of consciousness through sex magic, the technique of ecstacy used to achieve spiritual illumination and union with the god power. *Sejdr* means "heating" or "boiling" with sensual fervor and is related to "shamanism," itself derived from the Vedic *sram*, "to heat oneself to practice austerities." The term's deep antiquity is revealed in its Sanskrit cognate, *siddhi,* for "the miraculous powers developed by the practice of yoga," which originated in the Caucasian homelands of the Indo-Aryan race more than five thousand years ago.[1] Sejdr's mortal representative was a voelva, less a priestess drilled in the performance of ritual than a seeress naturally gifted in psychic power.

For her deification of life's highest, most wonderful impulse, the Christians condemned Mardal-Freya as a lascivious witch. But long before and ever since, Friday was named after her, even though Dark Age religious zealots declared the day unlucky: it belonged to the despised goddess, and the Crucifixion allegedly took place on a Friday, as well.

Her place in the Norse zodiac begins on the first day of spring, March 21, and runs to April 20. Known as Bilskirnir, or Lightning, it parallels Aries. Her color, red, symbolic of passion, is similarly appropriate.

Mardal-Freya's interest in the love life of men and women, together with her gift of Sejdr, exemplifies her rune. On a general level, it means human interaction and interdependence, aid or cooperation. Its energy inflects society, brotherhood, sisterhood, idealism, teamwork, civilized behavior, shared experience, social order, mutual support, collaboration, reciprocity, unanimity, and harmony. In short, the glyph deals with relationships, social and personal. When concerned with affairs of the heart, it is the rune of passion, desire, and sensual fulfillment. The magic it emanates is the mystery of love. According to Kunz, her gemstone, amethyst, "had a sobering effect . . . upon those over-excited by the love-passion."[2]

Reversed, Mardal-Freya's rune means we can expect no help from others; a definite lack of cooperation. Indifference and conspiracies surround our endeavors. More than one opponent threatens us. Opposition here is in the form of a group or alliance of people in common cause against us. Our personal relationships are seriously undermined, perhaps by our own selfishness. We have fallen into an alien lifestyle contrary to our inner truths—or we may be thrust into an environment or relationship that is alien to our concept of living the authentic life.

23

Loki

The Trickster

He was the strangest god in Asgard. His character was a contradictory brew of envy of and contempt for the Aesir he both helped and hindered with his tricks. When Thor's war hammer, Mjollnir, was stolen by one of Jotunheim's dim-witted natives, Loki devised a successful if demeaning plan to retrieve it. He dressed up the storm god as the goddess of love. Thus disguised, Thor posed as a bride-to-be for the giant thief. At the wedding banquet, Thor revealed himself, took back his war hammer, and vented his humiliation with a general massacre in Jotunheim.

Offsetting his assistance, Loki committed numerous crimes, such as conspiring to cut off the golden tresses of Sif, Thor's beloved wife. Her hair was eventually restored by dwarf craftsmen, who spun it from real gold, and it appeared to grow naturally once more.

Loki was angry with the Aesir, because they did not admit him into their fellowship. But it was his own unstable personality that caused them to keep him at bay. They both needed and despised him. When he conspired to commit murder, however, he went too far. For his part in the assassination of Balder, *heaven's* favorite son, Loki was taken to the summit of a remote mountain. There, the gods bound him on his back across three flat boulders. From the low branch of an overhanging tree they hung a poisonous snake. Venom trickled continuously from the snake's mouth onto Loki's face.

Like many wicked husbands, he had a compassionate wife, who some-how saw through all his evil ways to the pitiable child within crying for recognition. Her name was Sigryn, and she ran to her fettered husband with a bowl to collect the serpent's viperous dribble. Whenever she emp-tied it of the overflowing poison, a drop or two fell from the viper's jaws onto Loki's exposed face. And he writhed in agony, causing earthquakes.

Thus he and Sigryn suffered until the Twilight of the Gods. Then the serpent that for so long tormented him slithered off to join its fel-low monsters in the last great battle of the Aesir and Vanir against their enemies. The bonds that held Loki broke, and he satisfied his frus-trated revenge by leading all the forces of darkness against Asgard on Doomsday at the end of the world.

Because Loki is the master shapeshifter, his rune is emblematic of strong psychic abilities. Its appearance advises reliance on intuitive awareness, our inner voice, and affirms that we are presently under the guidance or influence of otherworldly powers. As the trickster god, Loki is in his real element when synchronicity enters human experi-ence. These meaningful coincidences are often mischievous incidents that prompt us to recognize certain spiritual connections weaving together the threads of our daily lives. Precognitive dreams, powers of the subconscious mind, instinctual knowledge, premonitions, telepathic occurrences, and related instances of paranormal insight are generated through his rune.

"The intuitive knowledge of the organic essence of the All,"[1] Guido von List writes of this rune,

> and therefore of the laws of nature, forms the unshakable founda-tion of Aryan sacred teachings, or *Wihinei* (religion). Such esoteric knowledge was communicated to the folk in symbolically formu-lated myths, for the naive popular eye, unaccustomed to such deep vision and clairvoyance, could no more see the primal law than the physical eye can see the whole ocean, or the unschooled inner, spiri-tual eye the endlessness of life in the All.[2]

Loki's glyph stands for strong memory skills and an ability to learn more. Inverted, it indicates deceit and overreaching ambition. Betrayal and misunderstandings are in the air. We have not properly read our own instincts. We are out of our depth and over our head in a project or dilemma beyond our powers to control or escape. Possibly severe difficulties are in the offing, because temptations or our own selfishness or laziness have misled us into imagining that we can somehow avoid the consequences of our evil actions. We sought to sacrifice right for an easy path, and we are forced to pay the penalty. Imagination has degenerated into self-deception. Guido von List warns that the reversed Loki rune can mean downfall and defeat.[3]

Loki's gemstone is malachite, because, according to Kunz, it protects wearers "from the attacks of venomous creatures."[4] His green-with-envy rune occupies a place in the Norse zodiac known as Thrymheim, the Noisy Castle, within Taurus, from April 21 to May 20. Thrymheim was the giant's fortress from which Loki rescued Iduna. Despite this heroic act, he was still forbidden to eat her golden apples of eternal youth. That refusal, while justifiable, nevertheless helped to set in motion the Twilight of the Gods.

24

Yngvi-Freyr

Patron of Increase and Prosperity

When the first Aryan peoples left their primeval homelands in what has since become known as the steppes of central Russia, they were engaged in constant warfare. The weather had changed—prolonged drought ruined their crops—so they were compelled to move on. A nameless horse-riding tribe, they were ferociously opposed at every turn by natives into whose territories they happened to unknowingly stray during their quest for a place to live. The Vanir god Yngvi-Freyr looked down on these hapless migrants from the celestial vantage point of Vanaheim and decided to help them.

He suddenly appeared at the head of their caravan, resembling a handsome man with a gentle though determined demeanor. He claimed to be a guide who would lead the folk wanderers north and west around dangerous opposition to a fertile, unoccupied country, where they could make a fresh start. Payment for his services would be demanded only if he successfully delivered them to the new land, but he promised his fee would not overtax them. They trusted Yngvi-Freyr, because he seemed to know his way around. Indeed, he did, and, thanks to his guidance, they were no longer confronted by angry warriors but instead proceeded on their long migration in peace and security. Eventually they arrived at a cool, green place that seemed most appealing. "Here we are," Yngvi-Freyr proclaimed. "Live and prosper!"

The god was true to his promise; the newcomers found the soil fertile and the climate mild. They celebrated their first harvest in fall, when they proclaimed Yngvi-Freyr their king, imagining he could wish for no greater reward. "There is one thing more," he told them. "To venerate the gods who love us and not lose contact with their will, set up a holy temple on that highest hill." A wooden building was raised on the most prominent place according to his wish, and this was henceforth recognized as the High Hall, still known today in Sweden as Uppsala. He instructed them in mound building, the heaping and landscaping of earthen sepulchres not only to memorialize the dead but also to concentrate earth energies for spiritual empowerment and transcendence.

After their first full year at Uppsala, Yngvi-Freyr declared that it was more proper for them to be ruled by their own kind, that they should choose a new leader, because he was about to resign. At his bidding, they erected a great burial mound featuring a single entrance and three holes. He entered, bolted the door behind him, and was never seen again. For some time his followers placed gold, silver, and copper presents into the earthwork, hoping to encourage his reappearance. When, after several years, they finally broke down the door and entered the mound, they found their gifts of precious metal, but nothing and no one else. It was then that they realized their first king had been no ordinary mortal, but a god.

To honor him and bless their posterity, they gave his name to their tribe. Henceforward, they were known as the Ynglings, and sired many generations of wise monarchs who, unless reason dictated otherwise, avoided violence in the affairs of their fellow humans. Once nothing more than migrants trying to find their way in the world, they formed the first royal dynasty of Sweden from whom all subsequent kings were descended. When conditions in Uppsala grew overcrowded, some sailed across the North Sea to an island on the other side of the continent. Here, as in Scandinavia, they established their kingdoms based on Yngvi-Freyr's peaceful principles. The Ynglings put down their roots in the new land and prospered, giving it their name by which it is known around the world: England.

During the ninth century, at the height of the Viking age, a *skald,* or poet, Hvini, composed the *Ynglingatal,* which sang of Uppsala's earliest kings, how they lived and died, and where they were buried. Four hundred years later the Icelandic writer Snorri Sturlusson based his *Yngling Saga* on Hvini's epic.[1] It is thanks to these works that so much of the Norse world has come down to our times, a legacy set in motion so long ago by the benevolent god Yngvi-Freyr.

Although he is better known today minus Yngvi, Freyr has always been revered as the patron of increase and prosperity who dispensed peace and plenty and was invoked at weddings. His regular sacrifice was the Froeblod, or Early Bleeding, a reference to the virgin bride's broken hymen on her first night of married bliss. *Froeblod* was a religious play enacted at Uppsala to dramatize the interrelationship among divine, human, and agricultural fertility. Yngvi-Freyr was recognized by three symbols: the horse; a magic boar known as Gullinbursti (Gold Bristling); and Skidbladnir, the Bright Deck, a ship large enough to comfortably accommodate all the gods, yet able to be folded up and tucked into a man's pocket like a handkerchief.

The horse identifies Yngvi-Freyr with the Ynglings in their early folk wanderings and all searchers compelled by necessity or misfortune to find new settlement. Gullinbursti signifies the rich harvest of golden grain that fertility engenders. Skidbladnir may refer to a moving stage resembling a ceremonial ship upon which religious dramas like the *Froeblod* were performed and taken from place to place. For convenient storage, it was perhaps folded away when not in use.

Yngvi-Freyr's twin sister was Mardal-Freya, and their relationship explains the configuration of his rune, composed of twin linked crosses. The god and goddess siblings symbolized, respectively, solar and lunar energies—male and female qualities, as they relate to fertility, or, in other words, sex. Of all the Norse gods, Yngvi-Freyr is most identified with the sun and its power to call forth life. He was the god of the Yule, a winter solstice festival regarded as the true New Year's day, when the light of the sun began to return after the year's longest night. Yuletide was so popularly ingrained in Norse culture that it could not be expunged by Christian zealots, as was done with most other examples of pagan spiritual life. Instead, it was appropriated for Christmas day.

Pennick states that, appropriately, Yngvi-Freyr's color is yellow, like sunlight, and points out that the god's solar fire survives in the English word *inglenook,* the corner of a fireplace.[2] Yngvi-Freyr's rune is one of the few that cannot be reversed; it has no negative aspects. It radiates success for the finalization of projects or plans. Worries vanish and present concerns evaporate like dew in the brightening light of a new morning. Like the Ynglings wandering from their desiccated Caucasian homeland, "this rune indicates the ending of an old phase of life to give birth to a new and more exciting one."[3] It implies relief arising from the satisfaction of bringing matters to a happy conclusion.

With his twin sister, he shares the same place in the Norse zodiac, Thryheim, the Noisy Place, from April 21 to May 20, corresponding to Taurus. Yngvi-Freyr's gemstone is ivory, from the tusk of his sacred boar, Gullinbursti.

25

Donar

Cloud Drummer

 Kyot was a lonely young man living at a time of spiritual repression. The old gods had been officially proscribed even before he was born. Yet within him somehow burned a natural reverence for the demonized deities of Asgard. His feelings were entirely his own, however, because to express them meant severe punishment, sometimes torture and death, always damnation. When in church, kneeling before the image of a man outstretched on a cross, he preferred to see not the foreign Jesus, but Balder, the earlier god of resurrection once worshipped by the Norse. Kyot secretly learned about the criminalized beliefs of his people from a poor old man—a loner, like himself—who remembered when Odin, Frija, Thor, Freya, Heimdall, and all the rest could still be revered.

The old man told him that the greatest valuable object from those days was a vessel that could expand its dimensions into a huge cauldron or shrink to the size of a small drinking cup. "Some said it originally belonged to the giants, from whom it was stolen by Thor for a banquet of all the gods in Aegir's palace beneath the sea," he recounted. "Others believed it was Aegir's all along. However the Aesir came to possess it, it was the real source of their greatness. The Gral furnished everything for those who claimed it for their own."

"*Gral*—What does that mean?" Kyot wondered.

"The Power."

As the old man shared his knowledge of an alternate spirituality, Kyot seemed transported to the lost realms of the Aesir and Vanir. He also learned about the runes and the conjuring spells that went into their creation. Anxious to explore their efficacy and establish some kind of relationship with the banned gods, he stole away from town early one dawn and reached a remote clearing in the forest. There, he selected an ancient oak that seemed to stand out from the other trees, and into its trunk he carved a single rune. He chose the sign of Donar, because his old teacher said it was one of the few magical symbols that possessed entirely positive aspects. If, in his first attempt at conjuring the god's energy, the lad made some mistakes, he hoped thereby to avoid any negative consequences.

He had just incised the glyph when he was startled by a loud voice.

"Kyot, you'll burn in hell for that!" He whirled around in time to be confronted by a black-robed figure who unexpectedly threw a fisherman's net over him. "I've caught you, you heathen devil!" the priest exclaimed, as he bound his terrified captive. "That evil gaffer who poisoned your soul has gone on ahead of you to perdition. Now it's your turn!" And he pushed the boy forward. Kyot stumbled and fell to the ground, but in so doing the dagger with which he carved the rune tumbled somehow into his hand.

"On your feet!" the man commanded. "You can't get out of this that easily! I've been watching you for a long time. The church sees and hears everything, especially a guilty conscience."

Kyot spoke not a word, but his mind was racing. Soon, he would find himself back in town, this time under lock and key to await some punishment he dared not contemplate. The priest railed on about the fine details of hell and damnation while he pulled the sinner along by a noose slipped around his neck. Kyot, meanwhile, worked his dagger up and down against the rope that tied his wrists. None too soon, they were free. With a desperate slash of the blade, he cut the rope around his neck. In another instant, he slipped his bonds and was off like a greyhound. Yet he could not completely disengage himself from the entangling fisherman's net, so he held it close to his chest as he ran for his life, and the priest's outraged threats echoed after him through the forest. For all his superior strength, the holy man was too well-fed to pursue the light-footed escapee with any hope of recapturing him.

Kyot ran all day, and for his first night as a religious outlaw, he slept under a spreading bush. For two more days and nights, chased by unrelenting fears, he ran and slept where he could, like a hunted animal, avoiding all contact with fellow human beings. The forest offered little that was edible, and he was growing progressively weak with hunger. Although he had long since severed the fisherman's net tangled around his wrist, he kept it and the dagger used to free himself, because these were his only possessions other than the increasingly torn and soiled clothes he wore.

During the morning of his fourth day on the run, faint from lack of nutrition, the forest suddenly ended, and he walked out into a broad field of high weeds. Storm clouds were gathering overhead, and he thought back to the god whose rune he carved in the side of an oak. "Donar!" he shouted at the sky with a mixture of anger and delirium. "I chose to make your sign, because it was supposed to be the most fortunate. But see how unlucky I am!"

Just then, a powerful boom of thunder sounded with such force that Kyot could feel it reverberate through his chest cavity. In response to this shock from the lowering heavens, innumerable birds, startled from their hiding places in the field, rose squawking toward the sky. The lad recovered from his astonishment sufficiently to cast the fisherman's net into the air as high as he could throw it. The mesh came down, entrapping no less than nine plump pheasants and grouse. He ate well at last, and thanked the god for the blessing.

The next day, Kyot crossed the field, soon after arriving at a small village where he traded the remaining birds for some new clothes. On the wall of a tailor's shop hung the portrait of a young woman set in a wooden frame covered with runic writing. Just as he was about to leave, Kyot mentioned in passing, "Gerda is a name as beautiful as her face. I am sorry to learn she died so young. But at least Friedstein is a peaceful place for burial."

The tailor was deeply affected by the boy's revelation. "You understand the runes, then! No one has been able to read them for at least three generations. You say her name is Gerda? That was my grandmother, and no one ever knew what became of her or where she might be buried. This portrait is an heirloom, but the identity of the person depicted here was always a mystery, until now. You have done my family an invaluable service!"

Kyot easily translated the rest of the inscription, which revealed much more about the tailor's missing grandmother. Henceforward, the educated stranger was made to feel very much at home in the little village, where he earned a modest living through his ability to read old runic writing still found in important documents, especially those pertaining to land and legacies. He supplemented his income by entertaining at banquets with the stories he learned from his old teacher about the gods and goddesses, dwarves and giants of the Viking age, for, luckily, in this village at least, such tales made for safe entertainment. His origins were never questioned or discovered by the villagers, who respected his learning and gentleness even after something of his renown spread beyond the area.

By then, he was himself an old man, still spinning his tales of Odin and the rest, when he was sought out by a curious visitor. The youthful scholar was aware of Kyot's reputation, and he wanted to learn the old man's entire repertoire of myths. One particularly fascinated him: the story of the Vessel of Increase, the Power known as the Gral. Kyot shared with him the entire account: he described the cup's infinite abundance and mystical potency, its strange disappearance, and the quest undertaken to recover it for the benefit of all humankind.

Sometime after the visitor left, Kyot passed away peacefully in his sleep, and he was mourned by the villagers whose lives had been enriched through his mind and heart. Yet his story of the Vessel of Increase did not die with him. For the young man who sat at his feet to hear the tale was none other than Wolfram von Eschenbach, the medieval author of *Parsifal,* the story of the Holy Grail.

Donar was the elder, less famous brother (some said, incarnation) of Thor, whose war hammer, Mjollnir, flashed lightning when thrown through the air. At such moments, out of sheer exuberance, Donar struck storm heads with his massive club, like a gigantic stick beating a drum, to generate thunder and force the clouds to give up their beneficial rains for life on Earth. Even today, the German word for "thunder" is *Donner,* and Thursday is Donnerstag. He was at once a god of agriculture and war, granting success in both undertakings—crops from one and spoils from the other. Donar was the deified personification of abundant increase and burgeoning potential in all manner of endeavor. These qualities are clearly expressed in his rune, which signifies growth and the activation of inner powers necessary to reverse unfavorable conditions.

There is a joy in strength associated with the god and his sign—a gleeful, almost effortless smashing of all obstacles. His motto might be "Attitude is everything!" In other words, by merely emphasizing our positive aspects of ourselves and our situation, even if reason dictates otherwise, we strengthen ourselves for coming success.

Although Donar's glyph is filled with optimism and cannot be reversed or inverted, in the presence of entirely negative runes it warns against excessive worry, because such a self-defeating attitude only attracts additional negativity. His sign sometimes indicates that if we make the best of conditions beyond our control, our cause will triumph in the end. It may also signal a life-changing event, often of a spiritual nature, concerned with mystical illumination. Fresh beginnings and viewpoints can initiate a new, even life-transfiguring, phase as manifestations of personal, inner germination. Such growth is synonymous with an enrichment of mind and spirit.

The Donar rune belongs in Himinbjorg, among the life-giving rains from the Cliffs of Heaven, corresponding to Cancer, from June 21 to July 20, early summer, when thunderstorms rumble. Donar's color is sky blue. His "gemstone," fluorite, is a transparent, crystalline mineral displaying numerous colors and perfect cleavage—all embodying the positive qualities of his life-supporting, auspicious rune.

26

Ostara
Goddess of Spring

Ostara Monday was the beginning of each year's most joyous holiday. It commemorated a time when spring passed into its fertile season as the earliest indications of new growth poked through the soil and budded on trees. Festivities began on the first full moon after the vernal equinox, when the spirit of the goddess Ostara returned to revivify the world (see color plate 7). Her companion was the moon hare who hid eggs, symbols of rebirth, for young sons and daughters—themselves synonymous with new life— to find among the fields burgeoning with first crops. Children collected the eggs and colored them mostly red, the color of life. For more generations than their poets knew, the Germanic peoples of northern Europe celebrated Ostara's arrival in festivities of gratitude for her yearly generosity. Her Ostramonath was a happy festival, but among the most important, too.

A time came, however, when the purveyors of a new religion visited the Northlands and achieved political power by converting tribal chiefs to the ways of their medieval church militant. All the gods and goddesses venerated for time out of mind were suddenly condemned, their worship forbidden under stern laws. Despite these Dark Age measures, the popularity of Ostramonath could not be suppressed. The churchmen appropriated all its symbols and set up an alternative Easter Sunday, when the traditional celebrating was officially allowed to venerate not the return of a "pagan witch," but the resurrection of Jesus. In the process of religious transformation, Ostara's moon hare was trivialized into an Easter bunny, and the creature's hidden annual symbols of rebirth were reduced to the subjects of a juvenile egg hunt. The reappearance of life was no longer associated with the goddess, the mother of all, but instead was attributed to Christ crucified. Thus, in sadly debased form, Ostramonath, unlike most Norse ceremonies, still survives.

On a material level, Ostara's rune describes valuable personal possessions, especially real estate, buildings, legacies, wills, or inheritances. But it may also refer to inheritances of another kind: the common legacy of a particular culture to which we belong or the unique genetic traits of the people from which we are descended. The structure that her glyph most often defines is the home, commonly our most important investment but, at the same time, something we often intend to pass down to future generations.

These extramaterialist considerations lead to another aspect of her rune: ancestry—in other words, that which we inherit beyond money, property, and physical possessions. Her rune addresses the value of blood. The wealth implied by Ostara is usually the kind that may be received and handed down, but not cashed in, bartered, or sold. Consequently, Ostara reminds us of our traditions, origins, even karma—the inheritance of the past that creates our sense of identity and place or rootedness in this world.

Reversed, Ostara's rune does not necessarily mean the loss of important possessions or disenchantment with our cultural and folkish backgrounds. It signifies instead that we may not expect any assistance from family or people of our own culture or tribe. We are abandoned, left to our own resources without the possibility of outside help. It stresses our self-reliance but warns that we are in danger of becoming greedy and materialistic and thus must restore a more balanced relationship between our financial and spiritual values.

Ostara's place in the Norse zodiac is framed between May 29 and

June 14, within Gemini, known as Sessrumnir in Folkvanger, or the Field of the Folk, which emphasizes her stress on shared cultural and racial values. Her color is yellow for the vernal sunlight bestowed on the world each year. Ostara's "gemstone" is the mineral petrified wood, symbol of the eternal character of life, which she personifies.

27

Current and Past-Life Rune Readings Using the Runes of the Gods

As described in chapter 2, the runes were invented during the early European Stone Age to signify spiritual energies personified in specific deities, and only much later, several centuries before Viking times—about two millennia ago—were they used as characters in a system of writing. Even then, they served both mundane and otherworldly purposes, particularly in divination. It is chiefly this predictive function that accounts for the resurgence of their popularity today.

Traditionally, the runes were believed to delineate patterns or influences that typically led to several possible outcomes, which the querent was usually able to anticipate, alter, or even avert through the exercise of free will. The future, as an accumulating force of events, did not appear invariably immutable to rune masters, but was more often pliant, susceptible to manipulation within reason. Relatively few impending incidents seemed beyond the power to change. Time was not sharply divided into past, present, and future but instead was regarded as a flowing unity that only appeared thus segmented from our temporal perspective. That which is to come is not a thing in itself but is an extension of ongoing, prior forces.

To determine the subtle course of future occurrences, so-called spreads were devised to allow the runes an opportunity to reveal certain themes interpreted by a hierophant or mystagogue who was familiar with the significance of each individual glyph and its identification with a specific deity. Variant spreads were and are many in style and sophistication, but all are derived from three simple layouts that still operate with a maximum of efficiency and a minimum of complexity. Rune-reading was a ritual. Its purpose was temporarily to remove the querent from the precinct of time into the realm of eternity, a transformation possible only by personal participation in myth. Hence, the immortals symbolized by the runes. Working with the runes was and still is a genuine mystical experience, because they enable practitioners to establish a personal connection with the gods—those personifications of the pervasive consciousness that orders the universe.

Each rune cast, whatever its configuration, was preceded by a two-step process. Prayers to and/or storytelling about the gods and goddesses set the emotional stage for the mystical drama that followed. Guidance and truth, no matter how unpleasant they might be, were sought from the deities, to whom were offered modest sacrifices (libations of water, food tossed into a fire, a semiprecious stone dropped into the sea, etc.) as expressions of sincere intent and gratitude on the part of those involved in the readings. These readings were primarily concerned with present events and those in the immediate future, or the progress and development of specific plans or projects. The querent, sometimes with eyes shut, randomly drew one rune at a time, ignorant of which glyphs were chosen. They were then sequentially laid out on a flat surface that allowed for every position, reversed or upright. The reader then interpreted their combined significance based on the qualities of the god or goddess represented by each rune. At the conclusion of these sessions, the deities were thanked for their assistance and asked for their continued direction.

Sometimes, to answer a simple, direct question, a single rune was pulled. When, for example, someone asked if he or she should undertake a particular sea voyage and the rune randomly chosen belonged to Ran in the inverted or reversed position, the querent was being advised to cancel or at least reconsider getting on board—but for a more specific understanding of what was to come, the layouts were consulted.

The most common is the Norn Spread, after the three Norse Fates who control human destiny. The first pulled signifies the past, Urd. Next in line to the right is Verdandi, the present. The last rune to the right signifies the immediate future, Skuld. A sample Norn Spread might read, from left to right, if all the runes are upright: Tyr, Vidar, and Erda. This indicates that the querent was not long ago involved in some difficult, even final, conflict or struggle from which he or she successfully emerged into the present. The appearance of the Erda rune in Skuld's position promises positive change, the happy outcome of everything that has come before. It could mean relocation to a new domicile, perhaps a dream house, because this glyph concerns matters dealing with land, real estate, personal properties, or environmental issues. On an individual level, it offers assurance for having taken the correct path—that the querent shall eventually reach his or her desired goal or destination, provided that he or she has the persistence and fortitude to keep pushing onward.

It affirms a feeling of our proper place in the world: an environment that nurtures the development of innermost truths and personal potential to fulfill them. It applies to particularly cherished interests or those things that give the most meaning to our lives. Marriage or marital issues—a felicitous union of man and woman—may also figure into the near future. The Erda rune is said to prevent injury from falls, so the querent may be involved in potentially harmful accidents from which he or she will escape unscathed. To assist in putting our spiritual vibrations in harmony with these positive potentials, the wearing or close proximity of turquoise or the color brown (earth hues) is appro-

Fig. 27.1. The Norn Spread

priate. Fulfillment of the Erda rune's promises may be anticipated under the sign of Aquarius, from January 28 to February 12.

While the Norn Spread is the easiest to interpret and affords an overall view of our time, it is also generalized and not as specific as might be desired. Nine, as described in chapter 3, was the Norse sacred numeral, and, as such, it was applied to a development of the triple layout. The Ennead includes six additional runes to provide more information about past, present, and future. Signs that appear above past, present, and future positions indicate favorable influences; those beneath are unfavorable. The querent randomly chooses one rune above, the next beneath each of the Norns in an alternating pattern, beginning with Urd, proceeding to Verdandi, and ending with Skuld.

Thus, as an example (using our sample Norn Spread as the basis for the Ennead layout), the Frija rune above Tyr indicates that the struggle in which we were recently engaged informs us that diligence and hard work achieved a certain level of material prosperity. The appearance of Sif's rune in the unfavorable position cautions us to prevent such new-won wealth from overinflating our ego. The Iduna rune above Verdandi means that the querent is experiencing an inner peace following the successful conclusion of his or her struggles, a tranquil moment that should

Fig. 27.2. The Ennead Spread

be used for meditation and calm consideration. Mardal-Freya's rune beneath the present position suggests that current success is challenged by the querent's love life. His or her personal relationship is somehow at odds with the recent acquisition of material gain.

But the Ran rune's appearance above Skuld emphasizes the forthcoming changes signified by Erda's rune in this position. The preceding Frija and Mardal-Freya runes defined the possessions and marital nature of those changes. The reversed appearance of Ostara's rune beneath the future position means that difficulties involving possessions and the querent's relationship with the beloved cannot be soon resolved but instead will depend for their final determination or settlement entirely upon the querent, with assistance from no one else.

To learn more about these developments, the querent may choose additional glyphs, using up all remaining runes, if necessary, and extending his or her vision as far into the future as the Ennead Spread allows.

The Agenda Spread's purpose is to define the evolution and outcome of specific plans or projects. Someone, for example, intending to build a new house randomly selects four runes, one after the other, in a circular pattern. The first rune selected signifies the querent's true intent, upon which the layout depends. The second selection is placed at the bottom, to the left of the first, and parallels the beginning of the envisioned project. A rune positioned opposite the "place of intention" (first rune) indicates a middle stage in development, and the final rune at the top stands for the culmination or final outcome of the project.

If the querent pulls a Balder rune, his or her intent is favorable, because the envisioned house is to be built on behalf of his or her family. Yngvi-Freyr's rune randomly chosen for the second position of early development means that the forces needed to undertake the project successfully are readily available. Donar's rune in the third position signifies an energy increase sufficient to carry the plan through the middle of its development. The Jordegumma rune in the final place promises a successful conclusion to all previous labors.

A Life Reading involves every Norse god and goddess, because they

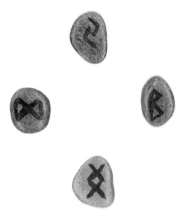

Fig. 27.3. The Agenda Spread

are deified personifications of all the spiritual energies that comprise our individuality. At least in general terms of the primary themes and strongest influences that help form a life, the entire course of an existence can appear from cradle to grave in this spread.

After completing either prayer or meditation dedicated to understanding our origins, early years, present condition, and future prospects, the Life Reading may begin. Starting with a single rune, the remaining twenty-three are subsequently laid out in an evolving spiral. This pattern mimics the corkscrewlike progress made by an infant as it is born from the womb. It is also associated with heliotropism, the tendency of plants to turn toward the sun under the direct influence of sunlight.

When completed, an overall view of the querent's early, middle, and final years appears. They are broken into six sections that correspond to as many sets of runes. In order of appearance, from beginning to last, they signify youth (birth to twenty years), adulthood (twenty-one to forty-four years), maturity (forty-five to fifty-nine years), and old age (from sixty years).

Interpretation begins by placing the first-drawn rune at the center of the spiral, progressing to the next and so forth until the last one is placed. If, for example, the first six runes drawn in a Life Reading are, in order of their selection, Yngvi-Freyr, Njord, Vidar (reversed), Thor,

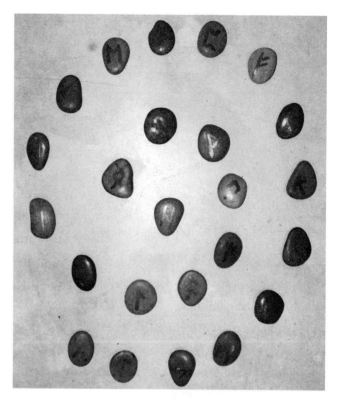

Fig. 27.4. The Life Reading

Donar, and Mardal-Freya (reversed), the querent was born into at least a moderately prosperous family. Choosing Yngvi-Freyr as the first rune is most appropriate, because it signifies birth, the breaking of light through the darkness, and bodes well for a successfully completed life. Njord indicates a difficult learning period in the very early years. Prolonged lack of success in resolving the problem results in unhappiness, as implied by Vidar reversed. But Thor suggests that persistence eventually overcomes the crisis, leading to new self-confidence inspired by Donar. Mardal-Freya reversed coincides with early romantic frustrations.

These new emotional storms carry over into the initial stages of adulthood, when the querent turns psychologically inward, according to Perchta. The querent's deeply personal frustrations make him feel unfulfilled in the delaying rune of Iduna. But from this introspection, he finds a creative spark, like Kvasir rummaging among the smoldering ashes of the hearth for inspiration. Ran reversed, however, means that the querent's inner turmoil erupts into misunderstandings, disagreements, and arguments with others. Ran's consort, Aegir, however, shows that these broils are the intellectually formative debates that mold the querent's developing character. Youth culminates, appropriately enough, with Jordegumma, who epitomizes cycles of growth and fruition.

The mature phase begins with a self-conscious, psychic awareness found in Loki. This intuitive insight is needed to see through the dishonesty and outright lies of Odin reversed that surround the querent. His or her struggle between an inner recognition of truth and the deceitful propaganda of the outside world initially results in failure, a sense of powerlessness, and shattered expectations. But some event or the appearance of a special person suddenly restores the querent's self-confidence in the form of the Sif rune. The gains he or she makes are temporary, as forecast in Balder reversed, and the querent's career outlook is grim, as verified by Frija reversed. Material riches, such as they were, are irretrievably lost, accompanied by deep disappointment.

With the transition to age, however, a major improvement in material and/or spiritual conditions takes place in the form of a legacy, as expressed in Ostara's rune. Although difficulties of the past still lay claim to the querent's happiness, as indicated by Ur-Nanna and Erda reversed. An important opportunity is missed, perhaps because of health problems, and the querent is out of sync with his or her surroundings. But these circumstances are overcome through Eir's perseverance, foresight, and direct action, bringing satisfying rewards from someone to whom the querent feels personally bound. Heimdall's appearance at the end of life is most appropriate, because he defines the absolute limits of our destiny in the physical world. As stated in his chapter, Heimdall's rune means that everything that happens to us—both positive and negative—is part of the process of life. His abode is Gladsheim, the Joyous Home of the gods, the next stop on the querent's soul journey.

The course and outcome of these spreads are not fixed, however, because we have been given free will by the Great Compassionate Mind that organizes the universe. The runes nonetheless correctly define the energies and patterns that typify our personality and lead us to our fate, as alterable as they may be. Character is destiny. To avoid a particular development of the latter, we must change the former. Fate is not entirely immutable, but it may be changed by the decisions we act upon in life.

Limnascate refers to linked spirals, a twin symbol adorning the most sacred sites in eolithic Europe, most famously at Ireland's New Grange and Malta's Hal Saflieni. The 5,200-year-old Irish funerary temple is oriented to sunrise of the winter solstice, an obvious celebration of sunlight's return after the year's longest night. Parallels to the soul's survival or return after death are implicit in the solar alignment deliberately incorporated at New Grange, or New Light, by its Stone Age builders. Although celestial orientations do not occur at the Maltese hypogeum, its identification as both the tomb and womb of the human spirit is nevertheless apparent.

The Limnascate design has been found in dynastic Egypt, Minoan Crete, Bronze Age Greece, and even pre-Columbian America. By far the largest specimen occurs in coastal Peru. It was etched perhaps two thousand years ago into the Nazca Plain, the driest location on Earth, where it marks the precise position of a subterranean aquifer; hence, the Limnascate's appropriate symbolism for a vanished people's life-and-death struggle with the encroaching desert.

In every surviving example, the linked spirals appear within a sacred context related to the passage of the human soul from one life to the next. As such, the twin spiral's function in rune casting for reincarnation research is deeply ancient, yet perennially appropriate.

The Limnascate must be preceded by a Life Reading. To determine the next incarnation, return to the pouch the first twelve runes from the twenty-four-rune Life Reading spread. Next, withdraw them randomly, one at a time. As each glyph is chosen, begin forming them into another spiral connecting with the first, until all remaining runes have been chosen. The spiral of twelve newly selected runes represents another incarnation.

If the querent wants to find leading patterns from his or her most immediate past life, the second spiral should be laid out to the left. A spiral growing out from the old one to the right signifies a future incarnation, the next one. The new spiral's twelve runes comprise an overview of the entire incarnation, not from rebirth to middle life only. The twelve new selections are divided into four sets of three runes each. As in the Life Reading, these sets represent youth (birth to twenty years), adulthood (twenty-one to forty-four years), maturity (forty-five to fifty-nine years), and old age (from sixty years). In a leftward layout, the first rune chosen begins with the last one of the most immediate previous incarnation. The randomly selected runes go back subsequently from death through old age, into maturity, then youth.

A specimen past-life spread of Vidar reversed, Ran reversed, and Donar reveals that the previous incarnation ended in frustration during a failed passage, which began well enough but ended in violent death. This final voyage was preceded by close comradeship and Aegir's protection, although Mardal-Freya reversed brought misfortune in love, and a period of hard training was demanded by Njord. Earlier, the well-to-do (Jordegumma) incarnation discreetly revealed an important, personal secret (Perchta), thus ending a period of frustration (Iduna), the consequences of which would nonetheless reverberate through the remainder of this life and into the next. During the querent's youth, he or she was creative (Kvasir) and cheerful (Yngvi-Freyr). At the time of the querent's birth, however, a sign or omen (Thor reversed) portended that he or she would eventually face great dangers brought on by the later, arrogant treatment of subordinates, behavior that appears to have led to his or her demise.

A Limnascate of twelve runes spiraling to the right from the Life Reading's last rune is followed in the same way to read a general outline of the querent's next incarnation.

The Buddha, when asked about the value of reincarnation, responded to the effect that knowledge of past lives is important only

Fig. 27.5. The Limnascate

insofar as we learn sufficiently from them to live our present incarnation in such a manner as to avoid karmic debt, for which we must pay with our next life.

Rune readings were sometimes copied in wood or stone, then used as the Norse version of mandalas: images for focused concentration and meditation to assist in the fulfillment of their prophecies. To simplify ready comprehension of the runes and their collective significance in a specific reading, each one was associated with a specific quality personified by its own deity (see chart on page 173).

Rune masters went beyond these superficial meanings to probe the more numerous, deeper meanings beneath these surface identifications, but experts at interpretation were distinguished from ordinary men and women not by any inherently superior piety or skills they might have had, or by special benefits personally obtained from some great teacher, but rather experience through practice and wisdom from meditation, paths open to everyone, enabled them to excel in a divination technique that connected them to the spiritual energies of our early ancestors. The survival and revival of Norse divination from those remote origins combine to affirm the enduring validity and power of the gods of the runes.

Frija	fruitfulness	ᛒ
Ullr	inner truth	ᚼ
Thor	luck	ᚦ
Aegir	influence	ᛉ
Ran	travel	ᚱ
Kvasir	creativity	ᚲ
Gefion	giving	ᚷ
Vidar	joy	ᚹ
Heimdall	delay	ᚺ
Njord	necessity	ᚾ
Iduna	inaction	ᛁ
Jordegumma	fruition	ᛃ
Eir	protection	ᛇ
Perchta	secrecy	ᛈ
Odin	wisdom	ᚨ
Sif	victory	ᛋ
Tyr	struggle	ᛏ
Balder	regeneration	ᛒ
Erda	true home	ᛗ
Mardal-Freya	love	ᛜ
Loki	Paranormal phenomena	ᛚ
Yngvi-Freyr	happy resolution	ᛟ
Donar	increase	ᛞ
Ostara	inheritance	ᛜ

Fig. 27.6. This list details individual runes and the quality personified by its deity.

Notes

FOREWORD.
THE RUNES ARE SPIRITUAL TOUCHSTONES

1. Thorolf Wardle, *Rune Lore* (San Francisco: Fields Bookstore, 1990).

INTRODUCTION.
CONNECTING WITH THE GOD ENERGY
OF THE RUNES

1. Thorolf Wardle, *Rune Lore* (San Francisco: Fields Bookstore, 1990).
2. Joseph Campbell, with Bill Moyers, *The Power of Myth*.
3. Guido von List, *The Secret of the Runes*, 57, 58.

CHAPTER 1. RUNE QUEST

1. Carl Gustav Jung, *Synchronicity: An Acausal Connecting Principle* (Princeton, N.J.: Princeton University Press, 1973).
2. Ibid.
3. Juliet Sharman-Burke and Liz Greene, *The Mythic Tarot: A New Approach to the New Tarot Cards*, Markham, Ontario: Stoddart, 1985.
4. Joe Fisher, *The Siren Call of Hungry Ghosts* (New York: Paraview Press, 2001).
5. Jamie Sams and David Carson, *Medicine Cards: The Discovery of Power Through the Ways of Animals* (New York: St. Martin's Press, 1999).
6. Chretien de Troyes, *Perceval: The Story of the Grail* (New York: D. S. Brewer, 2006).
7. Wolfram von Eschenbach, *Parsifal*, trans. Helen M. Mustard and Charles E. Passage (New York: Vintage Books, 1961), xlii.
8. Paul Belloni Du Chailu, *The Viking Age: The Early History, Manners, and*

Customs of the Ancestors of the English-Speaking Nations: Illustrated from the Antiquities Discovered in . . . from the Ancient Sagas and Eddas (New York: Adamant Media Corporation, 2001), volume 2, 155.

9. Frank Joseph, *The Destruction of Atlantis* (Rochester, Vt.: Bear and Company, 2002).

10. Paul Belloni Du Chaillu, *The Viking Age.*

11. Karl Theodor Weigel, "Woher stammen die Runen?" 269–74.

12. Murray Hope, "Practical Rune Magic," in *Fate* 38, no 3, issue 420 (March 1985): 88.

13. Ralph H. Blume, *The Book of Runes*, 25th Anniversary Edition (New York: Thomas Dunne Books, 2008).

14. Karl Theodor Weigel, "Woher stammen die Runen?"

15. Carolyne Larrington, trans., *The Poetic Edda* (New York: Oxford University Press, 2009).

CHAPTER 2. RUNIC ORIGINS

1. Karl Theodor Weigel, "Woher stammen die Runen?"

2. Guido von List, *The Secret of the Runes.*

3. Karl Theodor Weigel, "Woher stammen die Runen?"

4. Marija Gimbutas, *The Civilization of the Goddess, The World of Old Europe* (San Framncisco: HarperSan Francisco, 1991); Mary Settegast, *Plato Prehistorian: 10,000 to 5000 B.C. Myth, Religion, Archaeology* (Herndon, Va.: Lindisfarne Books, 2000).

5. William R. Corliss, *Archaeologgical Anomalies: Small Artifacts* (Glen Arm, Md.: The Sourcebook Project, 2003).

6. Ibid.

7. Mary Settegast, *Plato Prehistorian: 10,000 to 5000 B.C. Myth, Religion, Archaeology.*

8. Ibid.

9. Karl Theodor Weigel, "Woher stammen die Runen?"

10. Marija Gimbutas, *The Language of the Goddess* (San Francisco: HarperSan Francisco, 1989).

11. Ibid.

12. Karl Theodor Weigel, "Woher stammen die Runen?"

13. Heinz Aberger, "Zur Herkunft der Runen," in *Die Sonne* 12 (1935): 344.

14. Garman Lord, "Ancient Germanic I Ching, Your Future in the Runes," in *Fate* (November 1975).

15. Karl Theodor Weigel, "Woher stammen die Runen?"

CHAPTER 3. FRIJA, THE QUEEN OF HEAVEN

1. Horik Svensson, *The Runes,* 46.
2. Johann Wolfgang von Goethe, *Maxims and Reflections* (New York: Penguin Classics, 1999).
3. Guido von List, *The Secret of the Runes,* 50.
4. Horik Svensson, *The Runes,* 46.

CHAPTER 4. ULLR, THE GLORIOUS ONE

1. *The Nine Books of the Danish History of Saxo Germanicus* (General Books LLC, NY: Barnes and Noble, 2009 reprint of 1906 edition).
2. George Frederick Kunz, *The Mystical Lore of Precious Stones,* 73.
3. Guido von List, *The Secret of the Runes,* 50.
4. Ron McVan, *Temple of Wotan,* 219.
5. Lisa Peschel, *A Practical Guide to the Runes,* 37, 38.

CHAPTER 5. THOR, THE PROTECTOR

1. Plutarch, *Lives,* vol. 1, trans. John Dryden (New York: Modern Library, 2001.
2. Ron McVan, *Temple of Wotan,* 220.

CHAPTER 6. AEGIR, THE OCEANIC GOD

1. Nigel Pennick, *The Complete Illustrated Guide to Runes,* 135.
2. *The Oera Linda Bok,* trans. Howard Schnell (London: Truebner and Company, 1876).

CHAPTER 7. RAN, GODDESS OF THE SEA

1. Horik Svensson, *The Runes,* 50.
2. Joseph Campbell, with Bill Moyers, *The Power of Myth.*
3. Ron McVan, *Temple of Wotan,* 220.
4. George Frederick Kunz, *The Mystical Lore of Precious Stones,* vol. 1, 88.
5. Horik Svensson, *The Runes,* 50.

CHAPTER 8. KVASIR, THE DIVINE INSPIRER

1. Nigel Pennick, *The Complete Illustrated Guide to Runes,* 74.
2. Lisa Peschel, *A Practical Guide to the Runes,* 49.

CHAPTER 9. GEFION, THE SACRED BENEFACTOR

1. Horik Svensson, *The Runes,* 53.
2. Ron McVan, *Temple of Wotan,* 221.
3. S. A. J. Bradley, *Anglo-Saxon Poetry* (New York: Everyman Paperbacks, 1995).
4. Nigel Pennick, *The Complete Illustrated Guide to Runes,* 53.
5. J. E. Cirlot, *A Dictionary of Symbols,* trans. Jack Sage (New York: Philosophical Library, 1962), 52.

CHAPTER 10. VIDAR, CONQUEROR OF DOOM

1. Horik Svensson, *The Runes,* 100.
2. Guido von List, *The Secret of the Runes,* 52.
3. Ron McVan, *Temple of Wotan,* 221.
4. Horik Svensson, *The Runes,* 53.

CHAPTER 11. HEIMDALL, HE OF THE ECHOING HORN

1. *The Saga of the Volsungs,* trans. Jesse L. Byock (New York: Penguin Classics, 2000).
2. J. E. Cirlot, *A Dictionary of Symbols,* 50.

CHAPTER 12. NJORD, THE NEEDFUL

1. Lisa Peschel, *A Practical Guide to the Runes,* 59.
2. Ron McVan, *Temple of Wotan,* 221.
3. Guido von List, *The Secret of the Runes,* 54, 53.
4. Ibid.

CHAPTER 13. IDUNA, GATHERER OF GOLDEN APPLES

1. Ron McVan, *Temple of Wotan,* 222.
2. George Frederick Kunz, *The Mystical Lore of Precious Stones,* vol. 1, 78.

CHAPTER 14.
JORDEGUMMA, THE OLD WOMAN OF THE EARTH

1. Joseph Campbell, with Bill Moyers, *The Power of Myth.*
2. Horik Svensson, *The Runes,* 101.
3. Nigel Pennick, *The Complete Illustrated Guide to Runes,* 55.
4. Ron McVan, *Temple of Wotan,* 222.

CHAPTER 15. EIR, WOLF MOTHER

1. Ron McVan, *Temple of Wotan,* 222.
2. Nigel Pennick, *The Complete Illustrated Guide to Runes,* 56.

CHAPTER 16. PERCHTA, KEEPER OF SECRETS

1. Ron McVan, *Temple of Wotan,* 222.
2. Nigel Pennick, *The Complete Illustrated Guide to Runes,* 56.

CHAPTER 17. ODIN, ALL-FATHER

1. H. R. Ellis Davidson, *Gods and Myths of Northern Europe* (New York: Penguin, 1982).
2. Ron McVan, *Temple of Wotan,* 222.
3. Horik Svensson, *The Runes,* 58.
4. Guido von List, *The Secret of the Runes,* 52.
5. Lisa Peschel, *A Practical Guide to the Runes,* 33.

CHAPTER 18. SIF, THE GOLDEN-HAIRED

1. Guido von List, *The Secret of the Runes,* 53.
2. Ron McVan, *Temple of Wotan,* 223.
3. Horik Svensson, *The Runes,* 57.

CHAPTER 19. TYR, WAR GOD

1. Snorri Sturlusson, *The Prose Edda,* trans. Jean I. Young (Berkeley: University of California Press, 1954).

CHAPTER 20. BALDER, THE DEATHLESS

1. Horik Svensson, *The Runes,* 63.
2. Guido von List, *The Secret of the Runes,* 58, 59.

CHAPTER 21. ERDA, EARTH MOTHER

1. Guido von List, *The Secret of the Runes,* 54.
2. Ron McVan, *Temple of Wotan,* 222.
3. Garman Lord, "Ancient Germanic I Ching, Your Future in the Runes."

CHAPTER 22. MARDAL-FREYA, GODDESS OF SEXUAL ROMANCE

1. Barbara G. Walker, *The Woman's Encyclopedia of Myths and Secrets* (San Francisco: HarperSanFrancisco, 1983), 325.
2. George Frederick Kunz, *The Mystical Lore of Precious Stones,* vol. 1, 63.

CHAPTER 23. LOKI, THE TRICKSTER

1. Guido von List, *The Secret of the Runes,* 60.
2. Ibid.
3. Ibid.
4. George Frederick Kunz, *The Mystical Lore of Precious Stones,* vol. 1, 105.

CHAPTER 24. YNGVI-FREYR, PATRON OF INCREASE AND PROSPERITY

1. Bertha S. Philpotts, *The Elder Edda And Ancient Scandinavian Drama* (Oxford: Phillpotts Press, 2007).
2. Nigel Pennick, *The Complete Illustrated Guide to Runes,* 135.
3. Ibid, 60.

Bibliography

Arntz, Helmut. *Handbuch der Runenkunde.* Halle an der Saale: Schumann Verlag, 1944.

———. *Die Runen.* Stuttgart: Internationale Gesellschaft für Schrift-und Buchkunde, Weltschriften-Atlas 1, 1937.

Baesecke, Georg. "Die Herkunft der Rune." In *Germanisch-Romanische Monatsschrift* 22 (1934): 413–17.

Behrens, E. *Zur Herkunft der Runen und zu ihrer Verwandtschaft mit vorge-schichtlichen und geschichtlichen Schriften.* Leipzig/Straßburg: Sternsee Verlag, 1941.

Blomfield, Joan. "Runes and the Gothic Alphabet." In *Saga-Book of the Viking Society for Northern Research XII* (1941–42): 177–94, 209–31.

von Bülow, Werner. "Das Runen-Mysterium und ihr Zahlensinn." In *Frauen-Weckruf* 25, no. 12 (1934): 163–66.

Campbell, Joseph, with Bill Moyers. *The Power of Myth.* New York: Anchor Press, 1991.

Colum, Padraic. *Nordic Gods and Heroes.* New York: Dover Publications, 1996.

Crossley-Holland, Kevin. *The Norse Myths.* New York: Pantheon Books, 1980.

Dieckhoff, Albrecht Diedrich. *Einführung in die nordische Runenlehre.* Hamburg: Rossler Verlag, 1935.

Düwel, Klaus. "Runen als magische Zeichen." In *Wolfenbütteler Mittelalter-Studien* 5 (1992), 87–100.

Ellis Davidson, H. R. *Scandinavian Mythology.* New York: Peter Bedricks Books, 1988.

Flowers, Stephen, E. *Runes and Magic: Magical Formulaic Elements in the Older Runic Tradition.* New York: American University Studies, Series I, Germanic Languages and Literature, vol. 53, 1986.

Gimbutas, Marija. *The Living Goddesses*. Berkeley: University of California Press, 1999.

Green, Roger Lancelyn. *Myths of the Norsemen*. New York: Penguin, 1984.

Grimm, Jacob. *Teutonic Mythology*, 4 vols. Translated by James Steven Stallybrass. New York: Dover Publications, 1966.

Güntert, H. "Runen, Runenbrauch und Runeninschriften der Germanen." In *Oberdeutsche Zeitschrift für Volkskunde* 8 (1934): 51–102.

Hempel, Heinrich. "Der Ursprung der Runenschrift." In *Germanisch-romanische Monatsschrift* 23 (1935): 401–26.

Jones, Gwyn. *A History of the Vikings*. Revised edition. New York: Oxford University Press, 1984.

Knight, Sirona. *The Little Giant Encyclopedia of Runes*. New York: Sterling Publishers, 2000.

Koch, Heinz. "Die Entstehung der 16 typigen Runenreihe." In *Zeitschrift für deutsche Philologie* 66 (194): 12–15.

Kunz, George Frederick. *The Mystical Lore of Precious Stones*, vols. 1 and 2. North Hollywood, Calif.: Newcastle Publishing, 1986, reprint of the 1913 original.

Leach, Maria, ed. *Funk & Wagnalls' Folklore, Mythology and Legend*. New York: Harper and Row, 1972.

Liestoel, Aslak. "The Emergence of the Viking runes." In *Proceedings of the First International Symposium on Runes and Runic Inscriptions, Michigan Germanic Studies,* 7.1, 1981, 107–18.

———. "The Viking Runes: The Transition from the Older to the Younger Futhark." In *Saga-Book of the Viking Society for Northern Research* XX, no. 4 (1981): 24–66.

von List, Guido. *The Secret of the Runes*. Translated by Stephen E. Flowers, Ph.D. Rochester, Vt.: Destiny Books, 1988.

Magnusson, Eirikur. "On a Runic Calendar found in Lapland." In *Cambridge Antiquarian Society Communications* 4, no. 1 (1878): 59–104.

McVan, Ron. *The Temple of Wotan*. Idaho: 14 Word Press, 2000.

Moltke, Erik. "The Origins of the Runes." In *Proceedings of the First International Symposium on Runes and Runic Inscriptions, Michigan Germanic Studies,* 7.1, 1981, 3–7.

Moufang, Wilhelm. "Der Ursprung der Runenreihe des Futhark." In *Deutsche Erde* 4 (1933): 52–55.

Myers Imel, Martha Ann, and Dorothy Myers Imel. *Goddesses in World Mythology*. New York: Oxford University Press, 1993.

Neckel, Gustav. "Die Herkunft der Runen."In *Forschungen und Fortschritte* 9 (1933): 293.

———. "Zur Frage nach der Herkunft der Runen." In *Die völkische Schule* (193): 225–38.

Page, Raymond Ian. "Runic Links across the North Sea in the Pre-Viking Age." In *Beretning fra Fjerde tværfaglige vikingesymposiu* (198): 31–49.

Pennick, Nigel. *The Complete Illustrated Guide to Runes*. Boston: Element Books, 2002.

Peschel, Lisa. *A Practical Guide to the Runes: Their Use in Divination and Magic*. Woodbury, Minn.: Llewellyn Publications, 1989.

Philippson, Ernst, A. "Runenforschung und germanische Religionsgeschichte." In *Publications of the Modern Language Association of America* 53 (1938): 321–32.

Pittioni, R. "Zur Frage nach der Herkunft der Runen und ihrer Verankerung in der Kultur der europäischen Bronzezeit." In *Beiträge zur Geschichte der deutschen Sprache und Literatur* 65 (1942): 373–84.

Polome, Edgar. *The Names of the Runes*. Heidelberg: A. Bammesberger, 1991.

Salus, Peter, H. "On the evolution of the runic alphabet." In *Papers from the Fourth Regional Meeting of the Chicago Linguistic Society*, April 19–20, 1968, 202–7.

Svensson, Horik. *The Runes*. New York: Barnes and Noble, 1995.

Thorsson, Edred. *Rune Might: Practices of the German Rune Magicians*. Woodbury, Minn.: Llewellyn Publications, 1989.

———. *Runelore: A Handbook of Esoteric Runology*. San Francisco, Calif.: Weiser Books, 1987.

Tyson, Donald. *Rune Magic*. Woodbury, Minn.: Llewellyn Publications, 1991.

Weber, Edmund. "Ein Handbuch der Runenkunde." In *Germanien* (1936): 257–61.

———. "Die kulturgeschichtliche Bedeutung der Runenschrift." In *Die deutsche höhere Schule* 2 (1935): 680–83.

Weidmüller, Wilhelm. "Runen—die Urschrift der Menschheit?" In *Schrift und Schreiben* 6 (1935): 71–77.

Weigel, Karl Theodor. "Woher stammen die Runen?" in *Der Schulungsbrief* 2. Berlin: n.p., 1935.

Index

Page numbers in *italics* refer to illustrations.